THE WOOL INDUSTRY A GLOBAL HISTORY

COVERING TWO THOUSAND YEARS

THE WOOL INDUSTRY A GLOBAL HISTORY

COVERING TWO THOUSAND YEARS

ANTHONY BURTON

PEN & SWORD TRANSPORT

AN IMPRINT OF PEN & SWORD BOOKS LTD.
YORKSHIRE – PHILADELPHIA

First published in Great Britain in 2024 by
Pen and Sword Transport
An imprint of
Pen & Sword Books Ltd.
Yorkshire – Philadelphia

ISBN 978 1 39903 675 7

A CIP catalogue record for this book is available from the British Library.

Typeset in 11.5/15.5 pt Palatino by SJmagic DESIGN SERVICES, India.

Printed and bound in the UK on paper from a sustainable source by CPI Group (UK) Ltd., Croydon. CR0 4YY.

Pen & Sword Books Ltd. incorporates the imprints of Pen & Sword Books: After the Battle, Archaeology, Atlas, Aviation, Battleground, Discovery, Family History, History, Maritime, Military, Politics, Select, Transport, True Crime, Fiction, Frontline Books, Leo Cooper, Praetorian Press, Seaforth Publishing, Wharncliffe and White Owl.

For a complete list of Pen & Sword titles please contact

PEN & SWORD BOOKS LIMITED
George House, Beevor Street, Off Pontefract Road, Hoyle Mill, Barnsley, South Yorkshire, England, S71 1HN.
E-mail: enquiries@pen-and-sword.co.uk
Website: www.pen-and-sword.co.uk

or

PEN AND SWORD BOOKS
1950 Lawrence Rd, Havertown, PA 19083, USA
E-mail: uspen-and-sword@casematepublishers.com
Website: www.penandswordbooks.com

MIX
Paper | Supporting responsible forestry
FSC www.fsc.org
FSC® C013604

Contents

Preface

Having been brought up in what was then the West Riding of Yorkshire – and, as far as I am concerned, still is – the woollen industry was something I was aware of from a young age, even if the nearest mill to my home manufactured linen. Over the years I have written extensively about the industrial revolution and textiles, with specific books on cotton and silk, but it is only now that I have decided to concentrate on wool. But although I left Yorkshire in my early twenties, I have returned to an area noted for its woollen industry. For over twenty years I have lived in Stroud, at the heart of the West of England cloth industry. Quite early in my stay, I joined the textile group of the Friends of the Stroud Museum, but when the museum moved to new premises, there was very limited space for machinery. So, a new group was formed, the Stroudwater Textile Trust, of which I became an active member and was chairman for a period of years. The Trust was able to build up a collection of machinery, some of which is now on display and can be operated. It seemed that after so much involvement, it really was time to sit down and start on this book.

Over the years, I have visited textile mills and museums in many countries, including America and India, and received help and encouragement from many museum curators and helpers, too many to mention. I am grateful to them all – needless to say, any mistakes are entirely of my own doing.

Anthony Burton,
Stroud

Chapter One

The Raw Material

The obvious starting point is to be clear about what we mean by wool. The Oxford English Dictionary defines it as 'The fine soft curly hair of the domesticated sheep (and other animals)'. Although most of this book will be looking at the wool of sheep, the 'other animals' will get their place in the story as well. The definition goes on to specify wool as 'used chiefly in a prepared state for making cloth'. The next obvious question – when did wool start being used for making textiles – is not easy to answer. It certainly happened long after earlier plant-based textiles, such as cotton and linen came into use. There is evidence of cloth being woven in Egypt as far back as 3000 BCE. But the earliest textiles made from sheep's wool that have been discovered only date back to c.1000 BCE. These are from Scandinavia and were made from the fleece of quite primitive sheep, with long rough hair. Mostly we have only fragments of cloth, but a Bronze Age girl's skirt and top were found in Denmark. This does not mean that no woollen garments were made earlier than this, simply that no earlier examples have survived. But the quality of the wool used in these garments does suggest that woollen textile making was still in its infancy.

It is only much later in history that we start to get more solid information about wool and the cloth trade. In her excellent book, *The Merchant of Prato*, Iris Origo tells the story of the fourteenth-century merchant Francesco di Marco Datini. Cloth making is known to have taken place in Prato, a small city in Tuscany, since at least the beginning of the twelfth century. The street names tell of the work that went on there from the Via dei Lanaiuoli – the street of the wool merchants – to the Via dei Tintori, the dyers' street. It was in this city that Datini set up in business in 1383. He entered into two partnerships, one with a cloth maker, the other with a dyer. There was also a shop in nearby Florence where the cloth was sold. But his first requirement was to purchase wool of a good quality. The wool from the local sheep was coarse and unsuited for fine cloth, so he had to purchase from abroad. One obvious source was Spain, home to the merino sheep. They are thought to have originated in North Africa but by this time, they were an established Spanish breed, noted for the softness of the fleece. They were so valuable that Spain jealously guarded their monopoly of these fine animals. It was forbidden to take a merino out of the country, an offence punishable by death. However, most of Datini's wool was imported from England, in particular from the Cotswolds.

The Cotswold sheep, known as the 'Cotswold Lion' from *Brett's Colonial Guide* of 1883, a book designed for settlers in New Zealand with information on different breeds.

England too at that time had breeds offering wool of the very highest quality. The most expensive was the Ryeland, a breed that originated in Herefordshire, and as its name suggests was fed mainly on the rye grass of the Welsh borders. The Cotswold sheep – often referred to as Cotswold Lions – almost matched the Ryelands for quality, and the wool was especially noted for its whiteness, a valuable quality for a merchant in the dyeing trade. Datini bought English wool through Tuscan companies in London. They got the wool mainly from North Leach and Cirencester. One of these agents wrote to him in 1403.

> You say you have written to Venice to remit us 1,000 ducats with which, in the name of God and of profit, you wish us to buy Cotswold wool … in the next few days our Neri will ride to the Cotswolds and endeavour to purchase a good store for us, and we will tell you when he has come back.

In another letter of 1405, they report having had a successful buying trip: 'We went to the fairs and purchased some very fine, perfect, and good wool, at the cost of 11 marks. Please God these countries of ours will be at peace, so that trade can flow once more.' The records show that in 1397 he brought in 38,749 pounds of English wool through Genoa, some for his own use, but much of it sold on to other merchants. The wool would have been shipped out from London, where it was weighed and an export tax paid to the English government. There was a special Wool Quay on the Thames, later renamed Customs House Quay, where the customs were collected. It has one other claim to fame. For many years, the man in charge of the quay was the famous poet, Geoffrey Chaucer. The only known example of his handwriting is, very appropriately, a note asking for permission to go on leave to visit Canterbury.

Northern Italy was by no means the only area importing English wools. By far the most important cloth making region was Flanders, a medieval principality that covered an area that now includes the French département Nord, the Dutch province of Zeeland and northern Belgium. Major centres of the trade were Ghent, Ypres and Bruges. Something of the wealth of the trade can be gained by their magnificent Cloth Halls. Bruges' Hall remains largely as built but the Ypres Hall, begun at the start of the thirteenth century, was almost completely destroyed during the First World War, though it has since been restored. Given that the opulence of these buildings was paid for out of the profits made in large measure from the business of making cloth from English wools, it is no surprise to find that the English merchants who supplied the raw material also did very well out of the trade.

The Prato merchant had sent his agents to Cirencester to buy wool in the early fifteenth century and shortly afterwards work was progressing on adding to the magnificence of the

The Cloth Hall at Ypres, photographed before its destruction in the First World War. It has since been rebuilt.

church of St. John the Baptist at the heart of the town. It is the grandest of all the Cotswold churches, and much of its magnificence was paid for by local wool merchants and clothiers. The Garstang family of wool merchants financed the building of the chantry chapel that contains a splendid carved oak screen, embellished both with the family coat of arms and their trademark. At the same time, two members of the Weavers' Guild were responsible for the construction of the Chapel of Holy Trinity which contains an elaborate reredos. In the sixteenth century, the old nave was almost completely demolished and all along the sides of the piers can be seen the merchants' marks, indicating just who had paid for it.

East Anglia rivalled the Cotswolds in the wealth of its wool merchants and clothiers, and nowhere epitomises this more than the town of Lavenham that boasts the finest of the so-called wool churches. Among the leading benefactors was Thomas Spring III, known as 'the great clothier' – many wool merchants were also clothiers, which means that as well as selling wool, they kept some back and sent it out to local workers to be spun and woven. His coat of arms and trademarks appear in thirty different places in the church. Although today quite a modest-sized town, in the great tax assessment of 1523-6 it was ranked fourteenth richest in the kingdom, one place higher than the City of York. That wealth can be seen in the splendour of so many of its other timber-framed buildings, including what was once the Guildhall, built in the fifteenth century, that later became the Wool Hall. Yet there is today very little evidence that there was ever a textile industry here at all, unlike some areas of the Cotswolds. You do not have to travel far from Cirencester to find ample evidence in the shape of former cloth mills – in fact just 13 miles away, in Stroud, one mill is still at work. None of that remains in East Anglia, a subject that will be returned to later. One other emblem of the importance of wool to the medieval economy is 'the woolsack', the cushion on which the Speaker of the House of Lords has sat since the fourteenth century.

The market for wool fluctuated greatly over the years. So too did the nature of the wool itself. The Cotswold wool which had been so highly prized for making fine cloth had, by the eighteenth century become altogether coarser. Samuel Rudder in his *New History of Gloucestershire,* 1779 wrote that 'it was never fine in the memory of any man I have conversed with'. It seems that the original breed had been changed by the introduction of rams from Warwickshire. As a result, instead of being used for the finest cloths, it was relegated to medium quality, largely used for the uniforms for the army and the East India Company. Another factor that came into play that had a real effect on the whole of British sheep farming was the enclosure movement that began in the seventeenth century and gathered momentum in the eighteenth. This involved changing the whole face of the landscape, creating enclosed fields out of what had once been common land. This enabled larger landowners to make notable improvements in how the land was managed, with great improvements in crop yields. Agriculture was improved, but the poorer classes who had relied on the common land were left far worse off, and felt a fundamental right had been taken away, expressed in a popular poem of the time.

> The fault is great in man or woman
> Who steals the goose from off the common.
> But what can be that man's excuse
> Who steals the common from the goose?

Nowhere was the movement to have more dramatic consequences than in the Highlands of Scotland. It gave rise to the infamous Highland Clearances, where families were evicted from their old homes to make way for the new efficient farms. The better landowners found new employment for their old tenants, but others were ruthless in their search for maximum profits, and none more so than the Duchess of Sutherland, who had inherited a million-acre estate when she married the Duke of Stafford, one of the richest men in Britain. She had the power and the money to clear away the old system of small farmers to turn the land over to sheep runs, still a highly profitable business. Between 1809 and 1821 it has been estimated that some 15,000 Highlanders had been turned out of their homes, the old arable plots ignored and the flocks moved in. The Scottish poet Sorley Maclean published an essay on the Gaelic poems associated with the movement. Most merely bewail what had happened and write of the land emptied of people, but one (translated by Maclean) by John MacLachlan is an especially bitter one addressed to a landlord of the clearances, that begins:

> And when a spade of earth goes on you
> The country will be clean.
>
> Nothing will go on top of you
> But the dung of cattle.

No one knows quite when the first sheep appeared in Britain. They were certainly here by the time the Romans arrived, and other invaders may have added to the stock; the sheep of St. Kilda's, for example, were allegedly brought over by the Vikings. Certainly, there was a large sheep population. Over the years, selective breeding produced a wide variety of sheep in Britain, eventually reaching around forty distinct breeds, ranging from the long wools of the Border Leicester to the short fleeces of the Suffolks. The weight of fleece varies enormously. One Derbyshire farmer working in the nineteenth century was well pleased that his fleeces averaged 14lb. The record, however, goes to a South Devon ram, with a fleece that weighed in at a whopping 42lb. One can imagine the animal stepped a good deal more sprightly with that weight off its back.

The medieval woollen industry thrived on exports, but by the seventeenth century, the situation had changed dramatically. More of the wool was being used to make cloth nearer home, and cloth exports became more valuable than selling the raw material. There was a general feeling that it was, indeed, a mistake to sell any wool abroad as it enabled foreign competitors to make cloth to the same standard as the British. Until the end of the seventeenth century, many clothiers bought their wool directly from the farmers at shearing time. Over the years, however, as the trade expanded, they would either buy from middlemen – the broggers – or from important trade centres such as Blackwell Hall in London. Eventually, in 1662, a law was passed banning the export of wool altogether, which led among other things to a new trade for smugglers. It was, in any case, an unnecessary law, as wool exports were already in decline and would never again reach their former importance. By the nineteenth century, Britain was importing a good deal of wool, some of which came from new suppliers across the globe.

In 1788, the first convict ship set off for Australia. It was a long voyage and sheep were taken on board when the vessel stopped at South Africa to provide meat for the crew and their unwilling passengers. The sheep that survived were taken ashore. Other convict ships followed and gradually the flocks began to build, with the occasional addition of some sheep from India. They were not, however, very well adapted for the Australian climate. But in 1797, two British naval officers, Captain Henry Waterhouse and Lieutenant William Kent brought twenty-six Merino sheep from the Cape of Good Hope. They had a royal pedigree. Merinos had originally been given to Prince William of Orange by Carlos III of Spain, and in 1789 the Prince had sent a breeding group of two rams and four ewes to South Africa. Once they had performed their duty, the original sheep were returned to the Netherlands, but the lambs they had produced remained in South Africa. They were cared for by Colonel Robert Jordan, but when he died his widow sold them to the British officers at £4 per head, almost £800 each at today's value. This was a lot of money, and something of a gamble, which at one time seemed a poor bet. The voyage was plagued by bad weather, and by the time the two vessels that carried the flock, HMS *Reliance* and a supply ship, reached Port Jackson half of them were dead.

It must have been tempting to Waterhouse to sell the sheep at once, as he was made an offer of 15 guineas a head by a would-be purchaser, on the condition he sold the entire flock. He turned it down. Instead, he began breeding his own

A flock of merino sheep in New South Wales

flock from a property, The Vineyard, he had bought by the Parramatta River, in what is now New South Wales. In time, as the flock increased, Waterhouse was ready to start selling some sheep, including some to Captain John Macarthur, who had originally tried to buy the flock.

Macarthur was paymaster of the New South Wales Corps. The regiment had been formed in England in 1789 and soon had a somewhat unsavoury reputation. The commanding officer, Major Francis Grose, established military rule, closing down the civilian court and overseeing a lucrative trade in rum. The trade was so successful that the army regiment was universally known as the 'Rum Corps'. Grose's reputation was based very much on profit for himself and his fellow officers. Where it had been formally agreed that, as far as rations were concerned, the men of the Corps and the convicts should be treated equally, when crops were bad, it was only the latter who saw their rations cut. Macarthur was ideally placed to have access to land and convict labour to clear it. He was granted 100 acres on the Parramatta that he named Elizabeth Farm, after his wife. His reputation was certainly no higher than Major Grose's. He fought a duel with a fellow officer, and was accused of financial crimes, including extortion. As it was clear that, as the only court available in Australia was run by his fellow officers who were unlikely to convict him, it would be necessary to send him to England in 1801 to face a court martial there. His wife stayed behind to continue running the farm with the help of a nephew. When Macarthur arrived in England, the documents listing his crimes and the available evidence had all mysteriously vanished and the case was dropped. It turned out to be very much to Macarthur's advantage. He had been given a free passage to England, and he had brought with him sample of his Merino wool, which British manufacturers declared to be at least as good as any from Spain. That was all the stimulus he needed. He resigned his commission and returned to Australia, bringing with him nine rams and a ewe from the Royal Collection at Kew. Back home, he had a massive land grant of 10,000 acres of what was officially described as 'unoccupied land' – the native Australians who actually lived there did not count.

It was the start of the major Australian wool farming industry. In 1807, a sample bale of wool was sent to England where it was sold at a London coffee house for ten shillings and fourpence a pound. In 1813, the Macarthurs were able to send over a major shipment that was valued at £8,000, over £700,000 at today's prices. Throughout the nineteenth century, wool from Australia was fetching premium prices in Britain, and there was always a race to be first back with a shipment of the new year's clippings. The fastest ships were the wool clippers, of which the most famous is the *Cutty Sark* that entered the trade in 1883 and continued through to 1895. 'Fast' here is a relative term as her record-breaking voyage still took 65 days to reach England. By this time, the flocks in Australia had grown to around 100 million merino sheep, but that number fell drastically by nearly half during the drought years of 1895-1902. There were further fluctuations in the flocks, with a new threat appearing with the widespread use of artificial fibres affecting the demand for the natural product. Today, however, the flocks are back to over 70 million and supply half the world's merino wool.

The other southern hemisphere country famous for its sheep population is New Zealand, though it did not have a very promising start. Captain James Cook when he arrived in 1773 released a ram and a ewe, which promptly ate poisonous plants and died. More sheep were brought over but were mainly bred for food, providing provisions for the once thriving whaling industry. By the 1840s, however, the whaling industry was in terminal decline and farmers started importing sheep from Australia. The boom years for New Zealand wool followed when it represented a third of all the country's export business.

The big change came in the 1880s with the introduction of refrigerators on ships. New Zealand lamb was to become a regular feature on British dinner tables. Lambs are, by definition, not going to grow to old age, so the call was for a sheep that would provide both a good quality fleece and good meat. The first sheep were Merinos, but while their wool is of exceptional quality, they are lean and have poor meat quality. The first solution was to cross breed with British sheep – the result was a wool that was ideal for manufacturing worsted cloth while at the same time producing good meat. James Little, who managed a sheep farm in North Otago on South Island crossed a Merino with a Romney. The aim was to create an inbred half breed, one which would reproduce true to type. The result was known as the Corriedale, named after his farm. Other successful cross breeds followed. The result has been a successful New Zealand breeding programme that satisfies the needs of both the wool and meat markets. The sheep population peaked in the 1980s at over 70 million, but has declined steeply to just over 25 million today. In the earlier period, there were 22 sheep per person living in the country. If that seems remarkable, there is one place with an even greater ratio of sheep to human inhabitants.

The Falkland Islands have a chequered history. When they were first discovered by Europeans, the islands were uninhabited by humans. Over the centuries, they came under French rule, Spanish rule, Argentinian and British. In the nineteenth century, whaling and sealing were important and Port Stanley was developed as a servicing station for ships making the dangerous passage round Cape Horn. Not all the ships made it, but in an area without trees, they were a valuable source of timber. I visited the islands shortly after the war with Argentina, specifically to look at the remains of these old ships from the age of sail. Some had been preserved, pulled up into shallow water, roofed over and once used as wool warehouses. By the 1870s, sheep farming had become the dominant activity on which the whole economy of the islands depended. The population of the islands is small, currently around 3,500, a third of whom live in Port Stanley. The rest live in the farms scattered around the two islands. They are not farms as we in Britain know them, but self-contained small settlements, with a main house for the owner or manager, a few extra houses for the farm workers and usually a store supplying essentials. The number of people is dwarfed by the sheep, half a million of them. They are bred entirely for wool, which means that you do not kill off the lambs for meat. I discovered the 365 diet – mutton yesterday, mutton today and mutton tomorrow. They are comparatively small players on the world stage, but no country has ever been more completely dependent on one source of income. In recent years this has changed as the islands have developed fishing and tourism as additional sources of revenue.

Sheep farming depends on the shepherds who tend the flocks. In romantic literature, the life of the shepherd is idyllic. Christopher Marlowe's *Passionate Shepherd* woos his nymph, promising her a life of endless delights. His plea is:

> Come live with me and be my Love,
> And we will all the pleasures prove

He obviously has a lot of time on his hands, for he later makes extravagant promises.

> And I will make thee beds of roses
> And a thousand fragrant posies,
> A cap of flowers, and a kirtle
> Embroidered all with leaves of myrtle.

Sir Walter Ralegh was rather more of a realist, in his *The Nymph's Reply to the Shepherd,* she reminds him that the life of a shepherd is not really all about lolling around in the sun:

> Time drives the flocks from field to fold
> When rivers rage and rocks grow cold.

Very different is John Dyer's immensely long poem *The Fleece*, written in 1757. It stretches to four books and tells the whole story from the care of sheep to the completion of cloth. It is fascinating, not because it is great poetry, but simply because Dyer knows his subject, and it gives an insight into the life of an eighteenth-century shepherd. This must be the only poem that contains details of sheep ailments and their treatments. Here is a sample:

> Of gouty ails, by shepherds termed the halt:
> Those let the neighbouring fold or ready crook
> Detain: and pour into their cloven feet
> Corrosive drugs: deep-searching arsenic,
> Dry alum, verdegrise, or vitriol keen.

For page after page, he relates the life of the shepherd. Here is another small section about the dangers facing new-born lambs:

> Mark the quick kite, with beak and talons prone
> Circling the skies to snatch him from the plain;
> Observe the lurking crows, beware the brake;
> There the sly fox the careless minute waits;
> Nor trust thy neighbour's dog, nor earth, nor sky;
> Thy bosom to a thousand cares divide.

Dyer's shepherd had no time left for wooing nymphs and making beds of roses.

Many shepherds lived in cottages that were rented out to them by the farmer or landowner. The great engineer Thomas

Telford's father John Telford was a shepherd living in such a cottage in Eskdale in the Scottish Lowlands. Thomas was born on 9 August 1757 and three months later on 12 November, the father died at the age of just thirty-three. The widow and the baby were at once evicted to make way for a new shepherd and they moved just a short distance from their old home, not to another cottage, but to just a single room. There was no money to pay for a gravestone for the father, and the family had to rely on charity from her brother to survive. This must have been an ever-present worry for all families in tied cottages. Some were more fortunate, owning their own homes. W.H. Hudson in his book *A Shepherd's Life*, written at the beginning of the twentieth century, described the life of one old Wiltshire shepherd, known simply as John, who after half a century of shepherding was still in 1860 receiving the same pay of seven shillings a week that he had been paid when he had started work. That is the equivalent of just over £50 a week today. But he had his own cottage, where he could grow his vegetables. For the shepherd, out on his own all day, there was always another food source. Theoretically any animal or bird on the farm was the owner's property, but for many shepherds a rabbit that had simply strayed on to the land was fair game, and if his dog happened to come across a dead partridge, he was not going to leave it to rot in the fields. Hudson reported that whatever the law might say, the majority of shepherds supplemented their diet by poaching. It was a natural compensation for low wages.

The shepherd's life alternated between periods of comparative calm and intense activity. The cycle began when the rams were introduced to the ewes. Markers were often used in the form of colours painted on the rams that were transferred to the ewes when they were covered. It was important to ensure that all the ewes were to be impregnated as a shepherd's reputation depended on how many lambs were brought safely into the world. Success required that the ewes were in good condition both immediately before they were mated and afterwards until they lambed. This often meant providing supplementary feeding in winter. In her book *Labouring Life in the Victorian Countryside,* Pamela Horn quotes a Yorkshire farm worker, Fred Kitchen, describing feeding the sheep on turnips in winter, contrasting that with the idyllic view of his life:

> We have no picture of the shepherd in the muddy turnip field; of him and his lad sliding about in the muddy sheep-pen with skeps of sliced turnips; or the lad, bending down to clean out the troughs, receiving a gallant charge in the rear from a too-playful tup; or when snow and sleet swirls round their ears as they 'chop and throw' in defiance of foul weather.

Lambing season was a particularly busy time for the shepherd. On large farms with big flocks out in the fields, he had to be on hand 24 hours a day. The shepherd's hut is now only seen as a bijou holiday let, but then it was the shepherd's home, wheeled out into the fields where he had to stay with just a dim light for company for weeks on end. It was just as important to him as to the farmer to see there was a good, healthy stock of lambs. Many shepherds were paid a penny per lamb in the nineteenth century. That may not sound very generous, but for the Wiltshire shepherd quoted above, a hundred lambs would bring a bonus of a whole week's regular wage.

The next hectic period came with shearing, a collective activity for many farmers. Pamela Horn's book again provides a graphic description of the start of the process, where the sheep were collected from their upland pastures and brought down to the sheep wash. This account is from F.W. Brocklehurst of Sheldon in Derbyshire. 'The farmers highest up the village would start with their sheep about 8 a.m., having first taken the lambs away, and amidst a tremendous amount of bleating, gradually all the sheep in the village would be collected until over a hundred would be on their way'. The ewes were then dipped under the water and thoroughly scrubbed and cleaned. Once they were released, there was no need to shepherd them back to the different farms; they all headed off to find their own lambs. There was then a gap of about ten days to allow the natural grease to accumulate in the fleeces to make shearing easier. The actual cutting was done with hand shears, until mechanical cutters were introduced in the twentieth century. This greatly increased the efficiency of the operation and in 2023 a new record was set in New Zealand when Floyde Neal single-handedly sheared 540 Merinos in a 9-hour period. The old hand shearers would have considered this a miracle. After shearing, the fleeces would be packed as tightly as possible, ready for sale. This was a job that would later be taken over on the big farms by hydraulic presses. The price the famer achieved would depend on the type and quality of the fleece. This quality would, in time determine the quality of the cloth which it would become after going through many more processes.

So far, we have been concentrating only on the wool of sheep, but wool comes from many other animals and has been used for textiles in many parts of the world. I have a woolly hat that was brought back from Nepal for me by my daughter that has been knitted using yak wool. One of the longest traditions to produce woollens of an incredibly high standard comes from the southern Andes of South America. When the conquistadores reached what is now Peru in the early sixteenth century, their aim was, as it had been in other parts of South America. to get their hands on gold and silver. They were probably somewhat surprised to find that the metals, so highly valued in the west, were far less important and considerably less valuable than cloth woven from the wool of the native alpaca and vicuna. Textiles made from the wool of these animals have been found

Sheep being washed prior to shearing in the early years of the twentieth century in England.

that are at least 3,000 years old. During the Inca period, cloth was actually the main currency of the nation and certain types of cloth were reserved for the emperor and other high officials. The cloth intended for the court was woven by men and specially chosen women in closed societies. Cloth was valuable and a gift of cloth significant. There is a good deal to be said for valuing cloth above, for example, silver: the first is useful, the latter merely valuable for its ornamental qualities and its comparative scarcity.

The wool of the alpaca depends, like that of sheep, on the breed. The Hucaya, which is the most common, looks similar to sheep's wool and is generally used for knitting. The Suri

An illustration from a book written c.1615 by Felipe Guamán Poma de Ayde, describing his experiences in South America. It shows an Incan weaver at work using a backstrap loom.

has a fleece that hangs in long curls, is silky and is better adapted for weaving. All alpaca fibres are excellent for taking up dyes, hence the vivid colours found in Incan and earlier fabrics. The animals are no longer limited to their native South America, and in the twentieth century they began to be imported into the United States. There are various estimates of just how many there now are in North America, but it may be as many as 250,000. The quality of its fleece has been recognised for thousands of years in South America: the rest of the world has now come to recognise it as well.

Chapter Two

Early Textile Techniques

Although early textiles themselves do not often survive, there is far more evidence available on how they were made. Unfortunately, there is no way of telling, for example, whether a device for spinning thread was used for wool or some other material, but it seems safe to assume that the techniques would be either identical or at least use the same basic principles. There are a number of stages that must be gone through before the raw material can appear as a piece of usable cloth.

Before any work can be done, the wool has to be thoroughly washed and dried and the fibres teased out. It can either be dyed at this stage or when the cloth has been finished. However, the wool was mostly dyed early on, ensuring a deep penetration of all the fibres – hence, someone who is evil through and through is a dyed in the wool villain. Throughout the early history of textiles, dyes were mainly based on treating vegetable matter. It seems probable that the earliest dye known to be used was indigo that originally came from India but was in use in Egypt as early as Dynasty V, some 4,500 years ago, though the indigo plant was not grown and in common use in the Middle East until much later. Unlike most vegetable dyes, indigo does not need a mordant, a chemical such as alum that has to be added to release the dye and fix the colour. Woad was the other plant used for a blue dye, and has, in fact, the same active chemical constituent as indigo responsible for producing the colour. The actual dye is produced by a fermentation process, dissolving the dye in urine. A papyrus of c.2000 BCE comments on the effect of this process on the unfortunate dyer: 'His hands stink, they smell like rotten fish'.

There were two main sources of red dyes in the ancient world. The vegetable dye was madder, a native plant of southern Europe and Asia, which uses the root rather than leaves or petals to produce the colour. Cochineal was known in many parts of the world. In South America, it came from the *Coccus cacti*, a parasitic insect that as the name suggests feeds on cacti. It was later introduced into European dye houses. Similar insects were, however, also found living on the kermes oak that grows in the Ararat valley in what is now Armenia. The dye is made by crushing the insects to a powder.

Many other colours were produced in the ancient world. A bright yellow, for example, can be obtained from saffron, made from the dried stigma of the crocus – *Crocus sativus*. Alternatives could also use turmeric. Anyone cooking with either saffron or turmeric and unlucky enough to spill any on their clothes will know what a strong colour it produces – and how difficult the stains are to remove, even without a mordant. The most luxurious of all dyes must be purple, well known as the colour of imperial power in the Roman Empire, but available much earlier. There are records of purple-dyed wool from Ras Shamra on the coast of Syria as far back as 1500 BCE. The purple was originally made in Tyre, part of the Phoenician empire. It used the soft parts of the sea snail mollusc Murex, boiling it for up to three days in salt water. It was an unsavoury occupation, as the smell of the rotting bodies and discarded shells permeated the city streets. A less aromatic method of producing a purple was to dye wool with indigo, then scatter ashes over the material and work it in with the feet. It was then rinsed and grease removed using clay or fuller's earth, then placed in a pickling mixture. After that, the madder would be added to the pickling liquid. The purple colour would be either predominantly reddish or bluish depending on the proportions of the dyes used.

Dye works were often separate from other buildings where textiles were made and even in modern times, they had their own special character. A former mill manager, describing the dye house at his works, spoke of going in there and meeting a scene reminiscent of Dante's Inferno, with men naked to the waist, stirring the cloth in huge vats of steaming liquids.

Whether dyed or not, the wool was now ready for processing, starting by disentangling and aligning the fibres. It seems probable that the earliest workers in wool simply teased out the fibres by hand. In later years, the wool was either treated by carding or combing. The former used hand cards and involved pulling the fibres through two cards, studded with wire, to align them. The carder holds one card horizontally, teases out wool from the bundle of fleece and lays it on top. The other card is then pulled over the first, usually no more than five times to produce fibres suitable to take for spinning. The alternative method used was combing, which is slightly more complex. Again, there were two elements. The two combs consisted of wooden blocks that had metal teeth several inches long arranged in several rows – rather more like oversized brushes than combs. One comb was fixed vertically and the wool thrown – 'lashed' – onto it. The fixed comb was then placed horizontally and the second comb brushed over it with a circular motion, collecting the wool from the first. They were then changed over and the process repeated. The combs were heated on a stove at regular intervals, which helped to prevent the fibres from breaking. During this process, the long fibres were released, but the short remained stuck to the comb. The former were used for spinning worsted, and the shorter pieces for woollens. The name worsted is said to have come from the village of Worstead in Norfolk. The name is also applied to cloth woven from worsted.

The next step was spinning, twisting the fibres together to make thread, and here we have far more information on how this was done for most of the early period right up to medieval times. The earliest technique was possibly very simple, just rolling the fibres by hand, usually across the thigh, but the resulting thread would have needed to be wound onto something, even if it was no more than a simple stick. This developed into the spindle and whorl. The spindle is a stick with a weight, the whorl, at the bottom. In some cases, the spindle had a hook at the top. A length of fibres is drawn out by hand from a bunch of wool, and then caught under the hook. The simplest method involves paying out the fibres, while the spindle is dropped and allowed to turn, creating the twisted thread. The spinner uses both hands for the operation, but a variation had the bunch of wool gathered on a separate stick that could be fixed in place, so that the spinner had one hand free. This was the distaff, and as spinning was women's work, an unmarried woman became a spinster and the female side of a family tree is the distaff side. In some places, the woman would tuck the distaff into her belt and continue spinning as she moved around. This was apparently still common even in Dyer's day, as it gets a mention in *The Fleece*.

And some yet adhere,
To the ancient distaff at the bosom fix'd,
Casting the whirling spindle as they walk.

The drop spindle remained the principal way to spin any thread for centuries. It would eventually be replaced by the spinning wheel. Quite where and when the first wheels were introduced is a matter on which experts still disagree. Some claim it started in China, others that it had its origins in ancient Persia and the majority claim it began with the Indian charkha. Whatever its origins, the charkha is certainly ancient and is still in use in India today. The name simply means 'wheel'. The first stage in spinning is to create a 'pooni', a sausage-shaped bundle of fibres, wrapped round a stick. It is the equivalent of the material held on a distaff. The Indian charkha is turned by hand and is used to turn a spindle to which the material is attached. The spinner turns the wheel with one hand, and with the other hand draws out the fibres at an angle so that they wind spirally along the spindle, providing twist as they slip off the end. More thread is then released from the hand, drawing it out. Once that is completed, the spinner, keeping the threads taut, reverses the wheel, and holds the thread at right angles to wind it onto the spindle. Mahatma Gandhi saw the charkha as a symbol of the old India before colonisation and set up ashrams where cotton would be spun for basic cloth, known as khadi. I visited an ashram where many women were employed, all sitting cross-legged on the floor, beside their charkhas. They worked quickly and efficiently, and I was given a lesson in using the device. We Europeans are not used to working sitting cross-legged, but that was the least of my problems. To produce successful yarn requires steady movements and co-ordination between the hand turning the wheel and the one holding the cotton. Where the Indian ladies produced beautifully even thread, my efforts were hopelessly lumpy. The ladies were much too polite to laugh openly at my efforts, but several had to hold their saris over their faces to hide their mirth. This is obviously an efficient handcraft, but it is not a machine that can readily be used for spinning wool, only short fibres. It did, however, form the basis from which the European spinning wheel developed.

The European spinning wheel that worked in a similar way to the charkha was known by various names – in England as the great or Jersey wheel, in Scotland as the muckle, in Ireland as the long wheel and when settlers took it to America it became the wool or walking wheel. One difference that I would have appreciated was that the vertical wheel was mounted above a horizontal support so that the spinner can stand or sit comfortably and not on the floor. As with the charkha, the operation is not continuous – once a length has been spun, it then has to be wound on in a separate operation. This problem was overcome by the introduction of the bobbin

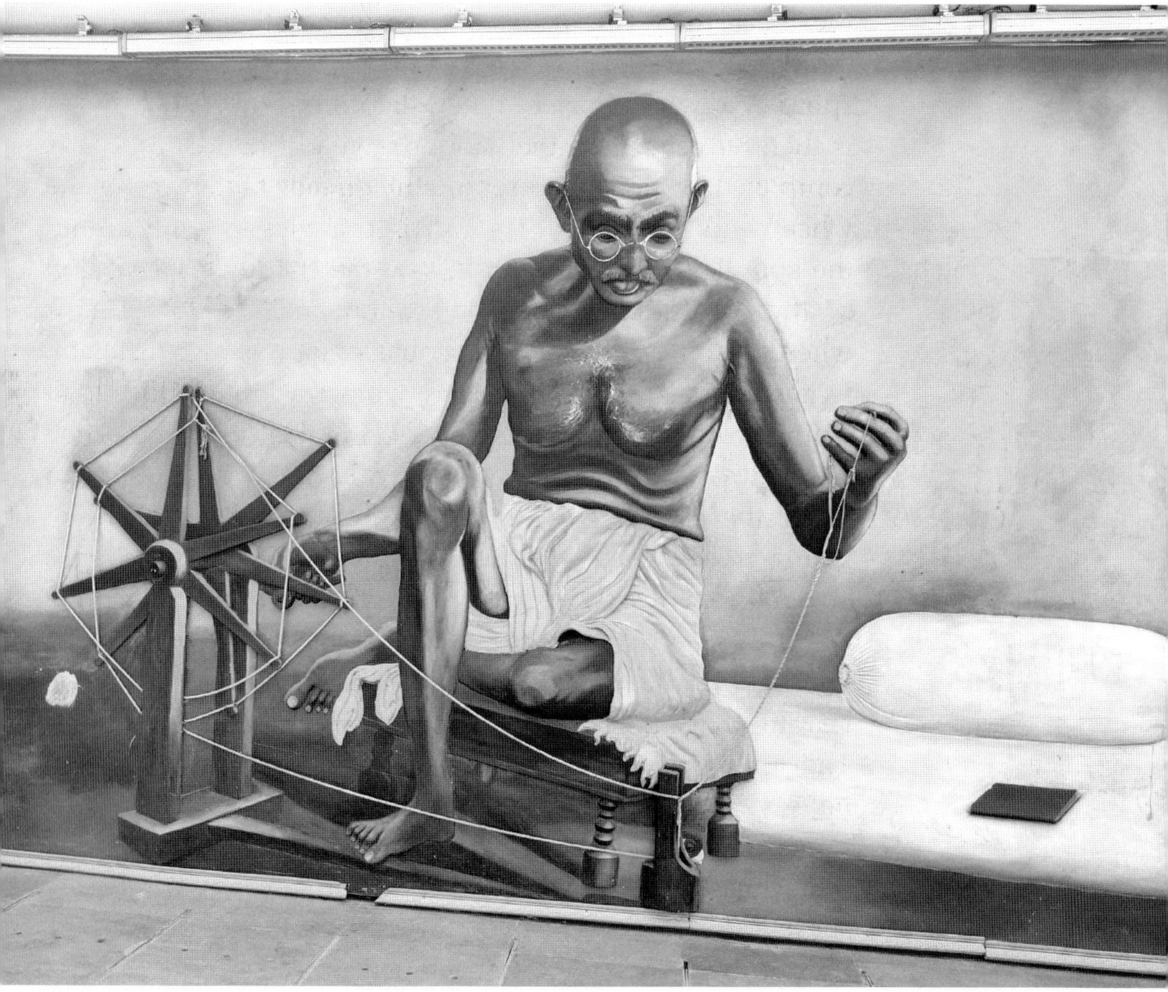

A painting of Mahatma Gandhi spinning with the charkha in the National Charkha Museum of India in Delhi.

and flyer. The bobbin was fastened onto the spindle that also had a U-shaped arm that fed the bobbin. The system works by allowing bobbin and flyer to move at different speeds so that, for example, when the bobbin moves faster than the flyer, it will be taking up the yarn. The mechanism works through a series of pulleys and a treadle was introduced to provide the turning, rather than having to move the wheel by hand. There is no positive information on when exactly the mechanism was first introduced, but there is a general agreement that the first known depiction of such a mechanism is in Leonardo da

Vinci's *Codex Altantica.* The treadle operated spinning wheel remained the principal tool for spinning wool until the end of the eighteenth century, and such wheels are still widely used today.

Once spun into yarn, the wool was ready to be woven on the loom. At its simplest, a loom is no more than a frame of some sort to hold the warp and keep it tight. These are the threads through which the weft thread, usually held in some sort of shuttle, is passed, going over and under the warp threads to make cloth. In the earliest looms, the warp was simply held taut between two rods pegged to the ground. Improvements were made. A short, flat stick could be used to divide the warp threads and could then be turned on its edge to create a gap – the shed – through which the weft, the pick, could pass. The warp threads were tied to a heddle-rod, placed above the warp. The shed stick was turned for the first pick, and the second by pulling the heddle-rod. Each pick was beaten down by a wooden 'sword'.

A very simple form of loom is the back strap, in which only one end of the loom is fastened to the ground; the other end is attached to a strap that is wrapped round the weaver's waist. In this case it is the weaver's body that keeps everything in tension. We know that this technique was in use in Peru when the Spanish arrived, thanks to an illustration in a Spanish book of the period (page 25). We have no means of knowing how long looms of this type have been in use, but back strap looms are still in use in modern Peru and, where in Europe handloom weaving before the Industrial Revolution had been men's work, in Peru it was and is mainly the work of women.

Early looms rarely survive. But they can be found in illustrations, such as those found on pottery. Two weavers feature in Homer's Odyssey and on ancient Greek vases; Circe, the sorceress who keeps Odysseus with her on her island, having turned his crew into swine, and Odysseus' wife Penelope, who, while he is away at the Trojan wars

A weaver using a horizontal loom, from a thirteenth century manuscript in the collection at Trinity College, Cambridge.

and making his way home, keeps would-be suitors at bay by telling them to wait until she has finished her weaving, which she never does. Both are usually shown using vertical looms, in which the warp threads are suspended from an upper beam, while the lower ends are fastened to weights, made of pottery or stone. Loom weights are regularly found on archaeological sites. Vertical looms remained in use in Europe until the late medieval period. Both horizontal and vertical looms could be modified by increasing the number of heddle-rods and shed-rods.

Eventually, the handloom became a more sophisticated machine. The warp threads were wound onto a beam, placed at the back of the wooden frame. They were then divided by the lease rods, where alternate threads are taken either over then under the two rods, or under and then over. This makes it easy for the weaver to identify any broken threads. They are then passed through eyelets in the heddle-rods, after which they pass through the reed, a device like a comb. The heddle rods are suspended from the top of the frame and can be moved up and down by means of a foot treadle. Alternate heddle rods are raised and lowered, leaving the shed for the shuttle to be passed through by hand, trailing the weft thread behind it. The reed is then pulled forward to the previous pick. As it grows on the loom, the cloth is wound onto a take-up roller. It remained more or less unchanged in Europe until the eighteenth century.

The handloom could be operated by a single weaver, unless broadcloth was being made. This was too wide for one weaver to reach across, so a second person, usually an apprentice or a son of the household was needed, to catch the shuttle and return it. John Dyer suggested that this was a delightful operation, though it must surely have been extremely tedious.

> Or, if the broader mantle be the task,
> He chuses some companion to his toil,
> From side to side, with amicable aim,
> Each to the other darts the nimble bolt,
> While friendly concourse, prompted by the work,
> Kindles improvement in the op'ning mind.

A simple device changed this necessity for a second pair of hands, the first fundamental change in the loom for centuries.

John Kay was born near Bury in Lancashire in 1704. As a boy he was apprenticed to a reed-maker. At that time, the reeds for the loom were made out of split canes. He recognised that wire reeds with loops for the threads would be an improvement and he began making them himself, travelling the country to sell them. Encouraged by his early success, in 1733 he began to think about other improvements. His first idea was to speed up the shuttle. Up to then, it had simply been passed over the top of the lower set of threads. He realised that the long board used to drive the weft home could be used as a 'shuttle race' and he added small wheels to the bottom of the shuttle to send it across the board. He then devised a system by which the human hands of the weavers were replaced by mechanical hands. Shuttle boxes were placed at both ends of the race containing 'pickers' that could be moved along short rods inside the boxes. These were attached by cords to a stick suspended in the middle of the loom. The weaver pulled the stick to one side, activating one of the pickers that hit the shuttle sending it across to the opposite side. Now the weaver could activate the shuttle over any distance, while still having one hand free to drive the weft home at each pick. It not only removed the need for a second pair of hands but speeded up the whole process. It became known as 'the flying shuttle'.

This was good news for the clothiers who employed the weavers, not so good for the families who found one of their members out of work. It was a simple device and easy to copy, which is what the clothiers proceeded to do, cheerfully pirating the invention with no payment to the inventor. Disillusioned, Kay left for France, hoping for greater success. He never returned to England and never made a fortune.

By the time, Kay had developed his flying shuttle, it was estimated that there were some 250,000 looms at work in Britain. Weaving requires good light and the height of the loom itself requires high ceilings. In an age when ceilings were generally low and glass expensive, this meant that the cottage weaver needed some sort of special workshop area.

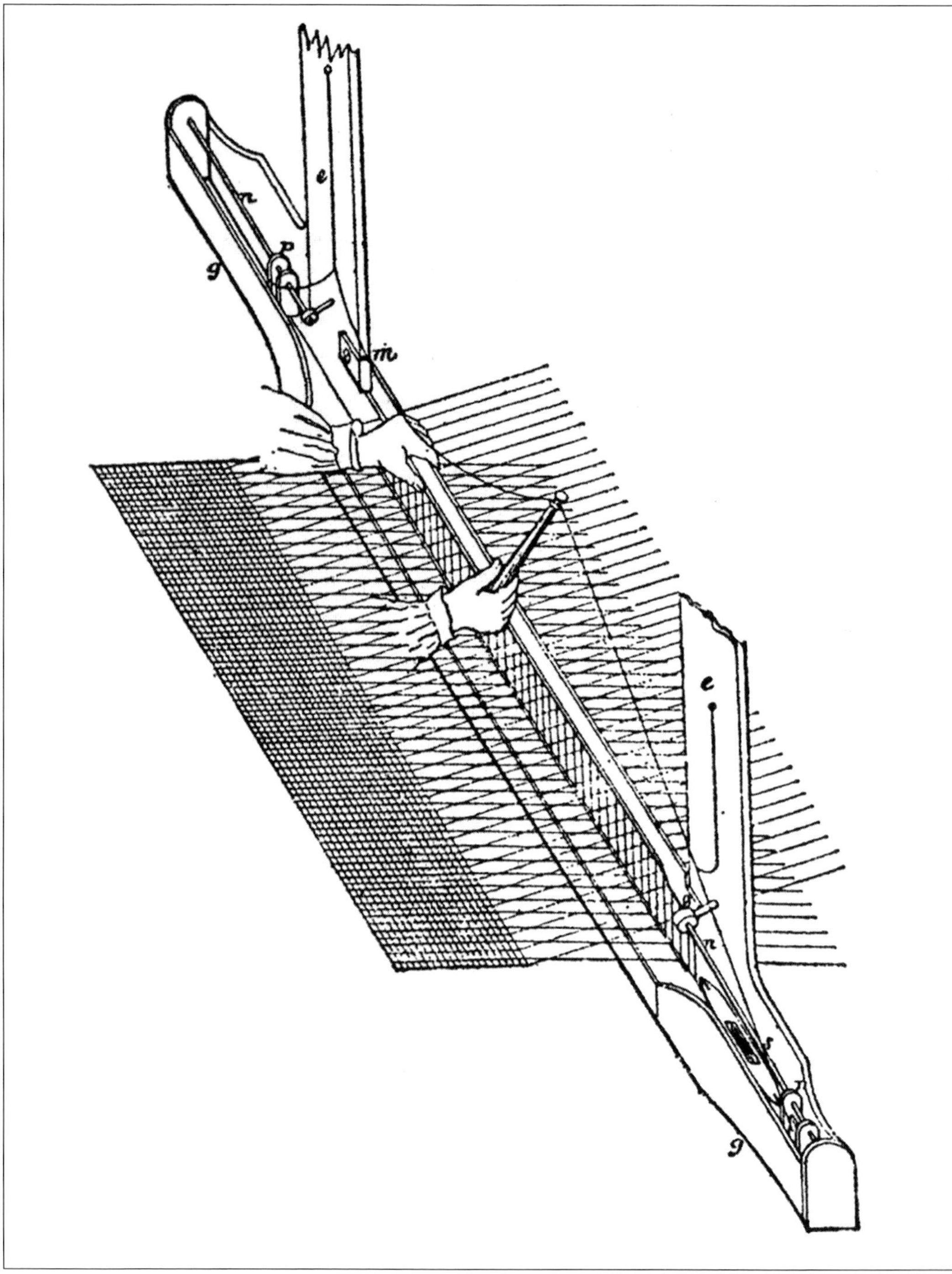

The flying shuttle from A. Barlow *History and Principles of Weaving*, 1884.

In some areas, these were separate buildings or lean-tos stuck on the sides of cottages. The most distinctive cottages had workshops on a third floor above the living quarters, with windows running the full width of the building. They can still be seen in cloth making areas of Britain as far apart as Wiltshire and Yorkshire. Traditionally, the whole family would be involved in cloth making. Downstairs, the wife would look after carding and spinning the wool with the help of the children, while the father worked upstairs at the loom. Daniel Defoe in his book *A Tour through the whole of Great Britain*, published 1724-6 described visiting a Taunton clothier who told him there were:

> … eleven hundred looms in the town … and not one of those looms wanted work: He farther added, that there was not a child in the town, or in the villages around it, of above five years old, but, if he was not neglected by his parents, and untaught, could earn its own bread.

This was not necessarily the family's only source of income. In rural areas, there was always a demand for extra hands at some times of the year, when the local farmers were prepared to pay good wages. A frustrated Wiltshire clothier had to tell his client: 'The remainder of your order shall be sent as soon as possible, but at present the workmen are in the fields hay-making.'

The cloth from the loom needed further treatments to remove the grease and matt the fibres. Originally, this was done by stomping up and down in a suitable liquid which, was usually stale urine. The tradition continued in Shetland among cloth makers as 'waulking', where the cloth was worked by teams of women using their bare feet, who accompanied the work with songs. When a piece of cloth arrived, it was the job of the leading woman to decide how many songs would be needed – and it was considered extremely bad luck to repeat a song when working a single

Scottish women 'waulking' cloth from an eighteenth-century engraving.

length. The songs would generally start slowly and then become brisker until the cloth was considered finished.

In the north of England, according to a nineteenth century historian of Huddersfield, this was the unsavoury process that followed weaving.

> The piece then made was spread on the floor. A large kilnful of urine and swine's dung was taken and strained through straw. It was then sprinkled on the cloth, and as may be imagined the smell in the house was horrible. As they lecked one piece it was laid down, and so layer on layer were placed, in the form of a long parallelogram raised from the floor: then all the members of the house got up and trampled it.

After that, the cloth was taken to the fulling mill. Fulling was the first part of the cloth-making process to be mechanised using water power. The water wheel was well established for powering grain mills and had been in use in Europe since the time of the Roman Empire – the first description ever written can be found in Vitruvius' *De Architectura*, written c.30 BCE. For many years, the water wheel rotating on a horizontal axle was known as a Vitruvian wheel. The earliest known fulling mill is recorded as being in use in France in the eleventh century, but soon became common in Britain, where it was also known as a tucking mill or, in Wales, a pandy. The wool was fed into a trough, with the fulling material – urine was still being used in the nineteenth century and other materials such as fuller's earth, a form of clay. The records of one fulling mill described how urine pots were kept for the workmen, but extra supplies could be brought to the mill, where they were paid for at the rate of a penny a pot. Perhaps there was a euphemism at the time – just going to earn a penny.

In the mill, the cloth was beaten by a huge wooden hammer with a curved head. Without the curve, it would simply keep hitting the same spot unless someone was on hand to move the cloth along. With the curve, it automatically shifted the cloth at each stroke. The power came from the water wheel that turned another wheel aligned with the tail end of the hammer. Projections were attached to the rim of this wheel. When one struck the tail of the hammer, it would push down the end of the stock, lifting the hammer head. As the projection cleared, so the hammer fell back down under gravity.

The fulling process could produce a certain amount of distortion in the cloth. To overcome this and ensure that the cloth was uniform, it was taken outside to tenters. These were wooden racks, some as high as 12 feet and many yards long. The horizontal beams were studded with tenterhooks, over which the material was stretched – which is why

Fulling stocks, from a nineteenth century engraving.

anyone feeling tense is said to be on tenterhooks. A very full description of the process was given in W. Partridge, *A Practical Treatise on Dyeing,* 1823.

> Were it dried without being fixed in a frame and stretched, the cloth would shrink up unequally, and leave it so rough and wrinkly that it could not be sheared without cutting, nor pressed with an even face. A cloth intended for seven quarters, being fulled into six and a half between the lists, is stretched to seven in the tenters, and is pulled in length, one yard in twenty beyond what is measured when it came from the stocks. When set in the tenters, stretched and

> hooked, the face is sprinkled with water, and then run from the last to the head end, first with fine cards, and then twice with long brushes.

As soon as it was dry, the cloth was taken down. A painting in Stroud Museum in the Park shows nearby Bowbridge in the eighteenth century, with rows of tenters spread up the hillside, many of which are spread with red cloth. This was the famous Stroud scarlet supplied to the British army – the scarlet still used for the ceremonial uniforms of the Brigade of Guards, though no longer made in Stroud. Tentering provided opportunities for the dishonest. The clothiers could stretch the cloth further than they should, producing a greater length to sell but at the expense of quality. If discovered, they could be fined. The poor might be tempted to steal cloth from the tenter. If caught, their punishment was more drastic. In 1779 Thomas Rudder was found guilty of stealing cloth from Frome and sentenced to death.

The next stage was cloth dressing. The nap had to be raised, usually by brushing with cards studded with teasel heads. Originally this was done by hand, but by the sixteenth century, the water-powered teasel raising gig had been introduced. This consisted of a drum, surrounded by battens into which the teasel heads were pressed. The cloth ran over the rotating drum, and a swivelling arm kept the cloth moving. One of these gigs, worked by an overshot waterwheel, is regularly demonstrated at the Stroudwater Textile Trust's site at Dunkirk Mill, Nailsworth. Once the nap had been raised, the surface could be smoothed by cropping, using large shears. This was highly skilled work – mistakes could ruin a whole length of cloth. The shearers were among the most highly paid of textile workers. All that remained now was to inspect the cloth and repair any small damages. After that it would be pressed and carefully made into bales ready for sale.

Setting teasel heads into a batten that will then be set on a rotating drum to raise the nap of the cloth.

Having looked at the different processes of manufacturing cloth, it is interesting to read accounts of how the textile manufacturing districts appeared to contemporaries. One of the earliest accounts was by a remarkable woman Celia Fiennes, who travelled through much of England on horseback

A cropping workshop: the central figure by the table is holding cropping shears and to his left, with his back turned, another man is using a teasel handle to raise the nap.

in 1695. Her accounts of what she saw were published under the title *Through England on a Side Saddle*. Here is her description of the thriving serge trade of Exeter:

> The whole town and country is employed for at least twenty miles round in spinning, weaving, dressing and scouring, fulling, and dying of the serges. It turns the most money in a week of any thing in England. One week with another there is £10,000 paid in ready money, sometimes £15,000 …The carriers I met going with it, as thick, all entering town with their loaded horses: they bring them all just from the loom, and so they are put into the fulling-mills, but first they will clear and scour their rooms with them, which, by the way,

> gives no pleasing perfume to a room … Then they lay them to soak in urine, then they soap them and put them into the fulling-mills, and so work them in the mills dry until they are thick enough: then they turn water into them, and so scour them. It is a pretty diversion to see it – a sort of huge notched timber with great teeth … The mill draws in with such a violence that, if one stands near it and it catch a bit of your garment, it would be ready to draw in the garment in a trice. When they are thus scoured, they dry them in racks strained out, which are as thick set one by another as will permit the dresses to pass between, and huge large fields occupied this way all round the town, which is on the river side; and then, when dry, they pick out all knots, then fold them with a paper between every fold, and so set them on an iron plate and screw down the press on them, which has another iron plate on the top, under which is a furnace of fire of coals – this is the hot press. The they fold them exactly, and then press them in a cold press. Some they dye, but the most are sent up to London white.
>
> I saw the several vats they were a-dyeing in of black, yellow, blue and green …They hang the serges on a great beam or great pole on the top of the vat, and so keep turning it from one to another – as one turns it off the vat, the other rolls it out of it; so they do it backwards and forwards till it is tinged deep enough of the colour.

Daniel Defoe, travelling just a few years after Celia Fiennes, also came to the west of England and stopped off at Bradford-on-Avon. 'The finest medley Spanish cloths, not in England only, but in the whole world, are made in this part. They tell me at Bradford, that it was no extraordinary thing to have clothiers in that country worth, from ten thousand, to forty thousand pounds a man.'

Something of that wealth can be seen in the local clothiers' houses, notably in the rows known as The Toreys on the hillside above the river. At the time he visited, this Bradford was bigger and far more important than Bradford in Yorkshire, though changes in the textile industry would later reverse their fortunes. But for the profusion of workers in the cloth industry, nowhere compared to what he found on a journey from Blackstone Edge to Halifax.

> We found the country, in short, one continued village, tho' mountainous every way, as before: hardly a house standing out of a speaking distance from another; and (which soon told us their business) the day clearing up, and the sun shining, we could see that at every house there was a tenter, and almost on every tenter a piece of cloth, or kersie [coarse cloth], or shalloon [cloth mainly used for lining], for they are the three articles of the country's labour; from which the sun glancing, and as I may say, shining (the white reflecting its rays) to us, I thought it was the most agreeable sight that I ever saw.

He was surprised to find few people about, but soon discovered that men, women and children were all hard at work in the cottages. His description of the clothiers' houses and their small plots of land, suggest they were not as prosperous as their counterparts in Wiltshire.

> Then, as every clothier must keep a horse, perhaps two, to fetch and carry for the use of his manufacture, (viz.) to fetch home his wool and his provisions from the market, to carry his yarn to the spinners, his manufacture to the fulling mill, and, when finished, to the market to be sold, and the like; so every manufacturer keeps a cow or two, or more, for his family, and this employs the two, or three, or four pieces of enclosed land about his house, for they have scarce corn enough for their cocks and hens.

Major textile areas such as these had markets in the principal towns, where clothiers and merchants could meet to buy and sell. The West Riding of Yorkshire became a major centre of the production of woollen cloth, some areas specialising in coloured broad cloth, others in undyed white cloth. The first cloth hall in the county was actually built in the hilltop village of Heptonstall in the middle of the sixteenth century. It is difficult visiting this delightful spot today to imagine it ever having much importance in the world. One of the few pieces of evidence of the old trade is the old packhorse route down to Hebden Bridge in the valley. But the arrival of water powered machinery and the construction of the Rochdale Canal led to the rapid growth of Hebden Bridge and the shrinking importance of Heptonstall. Leeds was to become the main market for a large surrounding area and by the 1770s was responsible for a third of all the wool exported from England. Originally the market was held twice a week in Briggate, one of the main streets of the town. Defoe gave this description:

> Early in the morning, there are trestles placed in two rows in the street, sometimes two rows on a side, but always one row at least: then there are boards laid across the trestles, so that the boards lie like long counters on either side, from one end of the street to the other. The clothiers come early in the morning with their cloth, and as few clothiers bring more than one piece, the market being so frequent, they go into the inns and public-houses with it, and there set it down.
>
> At seven o'clock in the morning, the clothiers being supposed to have all come by that time, even in the winter, the market bell rings; it would surprise a stranger to see in how few minutes, without hurry or noise, and not the least disorder, the whole market is filled; all the boards upon the trestles are covered with cloth, close to one another as the pieces can lie long ways by one another, and behind each piece of cloth, the clothier standing to sell it.
>
> By nine o'clock in the morning, all the deals had been struck and the whole market is closed and the boards and trestles removed.

Faced by competition from the market at Wakefield, the clothiers realised that to maintain their position they needed something better than a street market to sell their wares. The first white cloth hall was completed in 1711. The grandest of the cloth halls was the Mixed Cloth Hall, completed in 1758 – 127 yards long by 66 yards wide, with two ranges of buildings. It was demolished in 1890. No one was allowed to sell cloth in the great hall until he had served a seven-year apprenticeship, though the requirement was later reduced to five years. Today, one great cloth hall survives in Britain to give an impression of just how important the trade was, the Piece Hall in Halifax, with three storey buildings containing offices, set round the open courtyard. It is a thriving centre, but no longer used by clothiers.

We have brought much of the story up to the start of what has become known as the Industrial Revolution that began in the second half of the eighteenth century. But we have only looked at one way in which wool was used – for weaving cloth. In the next chapter we shall look at the alternative use of yarn.

Chapter Three

Knitting

The origins of knitting are a mystery. Why would anyone looking at a pile of wool think – if I had a pair of pointed sticks, I could use them to create a woollen garment? Weaving, by contrast, seems entirely logical – intertwining two sets of threads. Knitting is a far more complex operation. No one knows its exact origin, but the technique has been in use for many centuries in different parts of the world. The Victoria and Albert Museum has a pair of knitted socks that are thought to be possibly as old as the third century CE. They were designed for use with thong sandals, as is obvious from the illustration. They were not, however, knitted in the way that we consider usual today, but used a technique known as *nälbinding* that actually goes back thousands of years. The earliest examples, dated to c.6500 BCE were found in the Nahal Hemur caves in Israel. The technique is also variously known as 'one needle knitting' and 'knot free netting'. In this technique, the thread is continuously passed through each loop, rather like crochet.

The origins of two needle knitting are obscure, but it seems to have developed very much later, probably in the Islamic world of North Africa. Many readers might well already be competent knitters, but for those who like me have never taken up the craft, here is a brief description of the steps needed for a straightforward piece of work. The first stage is casting on a single needle. A slip knot is used to fasten the wool to one of the needles. The knitter then makes a loop of wool over a thumb, pushes the needle through and pulls the wool over the needle, then slips a loop over that to hold it firm. This is continued until there is an appropriate number

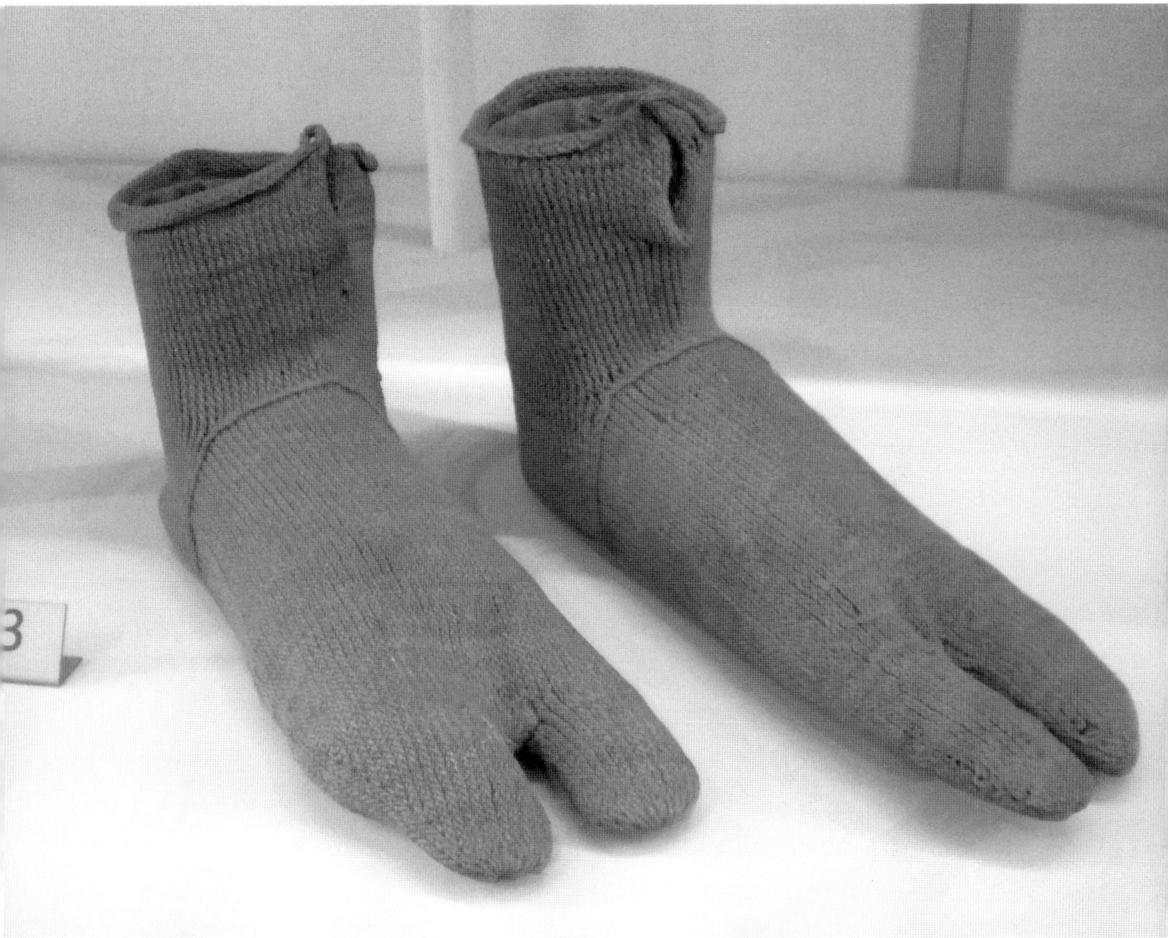

of loops on the needle. The next stage involves the second needle to knit the next row, starting with the first stitch on the original needle. For right-handed knitters, the original needle is usually held in the left hand. The right-hand needle is then passed through the front of that stitch, then yarn wound over the point of the right-hand needle. The yarn is then drawn through the stitch, forming a new stitch on the right-hand needle. The original stitch is then slipped off the left-hand needle. At the end of the row, all the stitches will have been added to the right-hand needle. The resulting knitted rows using this stitch will have a series of 'v's showing on the

A pair of knitted socks, designed to be worn with thonged sandals made in Egypt and now in the Victoria and Albert Museum, London. Their date is uncertain, but they could have been knitted as far back as 250 CE.

fabric. The other standard stitch is the purl that is, in effect, the reverse of the plain stitch. Combining the two provides texture for the garment.

Describing the process makes it seem remarkably complex, but in essence what the knitter is doing is making a series of interlocking loops. As no knots are involved, other than the one used at the very beginning, if a part is pulled a whole row can unravel. There is obviously skill involved in even the simplest knitting. Tension must be properly and evenly maintained throughout if the material itself is to be even. Knitters could produce patterned fabrics using different coloured wools and this was done in the early Islamic period. Shaping could be done in several ways: decreasing by knitting two together, increasing by pulling two or more over each stitch or by changing the size of the needles. Tubular knitting, for stockings for example, could be produced using four needles.

Knitting with two needles seems to have arrived in Europe in the fourteenth century. Professional knitters formed Guilds to regulate the trade. In order to become a journeyman an apprentice had to serve a specified number of years, and then produce work to demonstrate their competence. A Strasbourg apprentice, for example, had to knit various items including a cap, a pair of gloves, a jacket and a decorative wall hanging. One of the earliest official records of knitted ware in England is the Cappers Act of 1571 that decreed that all males over the age of six, apart from the aristocracy, should on Sundays and holidays wear 'a Cap of Wool knit, thicked and dressed in in England, made within this Realm, and only dressed and finished by some of the Trade of Cappers, upon pain to forfeit for every Day of not wearing three Shillings four Pence.'

Throughout the Yorkshire Dales, knitting was an essential activity, providing extra income for often poor families. Travellers such as Defoe commented on their speed of workmanship – speed that so impressed one visitor that he referred to the 'furious knitters of Wensleydale'. George Walker in his book *The Costume of Yorkshire*, 1814 described the life of the area and one of the women of Wensleydale – one can see why women such as her were 'furious knitters'.

> In any business where the assistance of hands is not necessary, they universally resort to knitting. Young and old, male and female, are all adepts in this art. Shepherds attending their flocks, men driving cattle, women going to market, are all thus industriously employed. A woman by the name of Singer, who lived in Cotterdale, was accustomed regularly to walk to the market at Hawes, a distance of three miles, with the weekly knitting of herself and her family upon her head, knitting all the way. She continued her knitting while she stayed in Hawes, purchasing the little necessities for her family, with the addition of worsted for the work of the ensuing week; all of which she placed upon her head, returning occupied with the needles as before. She was so accomplished and expert, that that the produce of the day's labour was generally a completed pair of men's stockings.

Further to the west, in Dentdale, the knitters were known, not as 'furious' but at the 'terrible knitters of Dent'. Where the Wensleydale knitters needed both hands free, Dent knitters often used knitting sticks, that were stuck in a waistband to hold a needle secure, so that only one hand was needed for knitting, and the other hand could be used for other tasks. Children were taught to knit from the earliest age, and if the parents were too busy to teach them themselves, then they were sent to cottagers in Dent as a form of unofficial apprenticeship.

The knitters of the Dales would have used a much wider variety of stitches than the two basics, described at the start of the chapter. Patterns were passed down the generations and taught by practical demonstration, not written instruction. Among the best known traditional patterns found in the British Isles are Fair Isle and Guernsey. Fair Isle itself lies off the Scottish coast, between Orkney and Shetland, so there may well have been a strong Scandinavian influence at work, as the islands were only passed from Denmark to Scotland in 1474 and many Scandinavian traditions survive on the islands. That has to remain speculation, but it is certain that the colourful designs have been around for a very long time. The knitting technique involves the use of double-pointed needles and a padded knitting belt. The garments are knitted in the round.

The Guernsey seems to have first been developed in its present form, when worsted wool was imported to the island from England in the sixteenth century. The sweaters were for use by local fishermen, tight-knitted both for warmth and to keep out the water. The patterns followed a general rule and had suitably nautical themes: ribbing on the sleeves represented a ship's rigging; garter-stitch panels were for breaking waves; and patterns on the shoulder were variously seen as ropes or seashore pebbles. When Sir Walter Ralegh became Governor of the neighbouring island of Jersey, he introduced Guernsey knitted items to the English court. Queen Elizabeth I liked the knitwear and it is said that Mary Queen of Scots was wearing Guernsey stockings on the day she was executed. As with Fair Isle knitwear, individual knitters introduced their own variations and it is said that bodies of drowned fishermen washed ashore could often only be identified by the patterns on the Guernseys. The idea of close-knitted fishermen's sweaters found its way to the Aran Islands off the coast of Ireland, where the locals developed their own distinctive sweaters, using cable stitching. Similar jerseys were knitted for fishermen in Brittany.

The earliest example of a book containing knitting patterns is *Natura Extenturata*, published in London in 1655. Knitting –

or netting as it is called there – occupies only a very small part of this huge volume. Before the knitting section appears, there are literally hundreds of unlikely recipes for equally unlikely ailments. The first of a dozen patterns is for a design called the Broad Arrow. There is no illustration just a description in words that begins: 'The first course at the beginning of the work is to make nine plain stitches and the tenth to winde twice about your pinne, and so to work throughout to every ninth stitch to winde the tenth.'

Knitting patterns only really became popular and were widely published in the 1830s. One of the pioneers was Jane Gaugin, and in one of her books, *The Knitter's Friend*, 1846, she made it very clear who her work was aimed at: 'That numerous and useful class of females, whose pecuniary means are limited, but whose minds and pursuits are well regulated and directed'. In other words, the patterns were not for women knitting as a hobby, but for those who needed extra income. Early patterns were grouped together in books, but in the early years of the twentieth century, leaflets for individual garments began to appear. They were first produced in Germany. Frank Mills, who was managing director of a Halifax woollen mill, was impressed by the idea, and when he returned home, he authorised Marjory Tillotson to recruit girls to prepare patterns. The first leaflet appeared in 1908 as the *Beehive Knitting Book*. It had a dual value for the firm – with luck, they would sell many copies at a small profit, but, more importantly, those who bought the leaflet would use their Beehive brand of wool. Later leaflets no longer had to spell out everything in words, but used accepted abbreviations, for example, s for 'stitch', p for 'purl'; psso for 'pass slipped stitch over' and so on. These instructions are now familiar to all regular knitters.

The outbreak of war in 1914 brought a new appeal for knitters. Lady French, the wife of Sir John French in command of the British Expeditionary Force, wrote a letter to *The Times:*

'There is a great need for knitted socks, etc. for our troops. I would ask those who have leisure to knit, or employ others to do, to send parcels as soon as possible'. The response went far beyond the readership of *The Times* and was answered by thousands who were certainly not in a position to employ others to do their knitting for them. Knitting clubs were set up in villages and towns throughout the country. Beginners were encouraged to knit simple items, such as scarves: later patterns were produced for other items, such as balaclava helmets and mittens. One of the odder patterns was for a chequerboard waistcoat that could be taken off during rest periods and used as a chess board.

Many of the women – and they were mostly women – who had taken up knitting during the war years, continued their knitting after it was over. Knitting patterns were widely sold and also regularly appeared in women's magazines. By now, home knitters had access to a whole range of different wools in a far wider range of colours than their predecessors had enjoyed. Yet, they were still using the techniques developed centuries before. Knitting machines became available in the twentieth century, but to see how they first developed we have to turn back to the sixteenth century and a curate in the village of Calverton in Nottinghamshire.

William Lee was born in 1563 and Calverton was one of many Nottinghamshire places, where knitters worked producing stockings. There are stories that set out to explain why a young clergyman should decide to devote his time to developing a machine to do the work of the hand knitters. The most popular, though certainly not the most likely, has it that he was trying to attract the attention of a young lady, but she was too preoccupied with knitting to listen to his amorous advances. He decided to devise a stocking-knitting machine, so that in future young ladies would be free to listen to the advances of amorous clergymen. A rather more plausible explanation is that curates were generally poorly paid, and if they lacked the essential aristocratic connections to acquire livings for themselves, were likely to remain poor. Young Rev. Lee could have seen this as a way of making if not a fortune at least a great deal more money than he would get from the church.

Knitting is itself a complex operation, and mechanising it presented difficult problems that had to be solved. In many ways, the knitting machine he devised had more in common with crocheting techniques. A row of hooked needles protruded from a wooden frame. These needles are never moved. Just as with hand knitting, a first row has to be cast on these hooks. The next thread is then laid next to the cast-on row. Thin metal plates, the sinkers, are arranged that were fixed above the gaps between the hooks. Above these is a moveable device known as a 'slur cock' that runs across the top of the row of sinkers, pushing them down one at a time – if they were all pushed down at once there would be a danger of breaking the thread. It is controlled through a wheel with ropes attached to treadles – the left and right slur treadles, so that once a row has been completed, the slur cock could be sent back in the opposite direction. When the sinkers were lowered, they pushed the thread down to form a series of kinks. The sinkers were now moved forward, carrying both the loops and the kinked thread, pushing them into the hook to create a stitch. Now a real problem occurred. If the sinker was simply moved back, it would unravel the stitch. Lee's answer was to provide another metal plate, the presser, that descended onto the needle hook to close it, grasping the stitch and allowing the sinker to be withdrawn. The needles were made of steel, and once the presser had been lifted, the hook would spring back into the open position. The control of these movements was through handles on each side of the frame. In time, the frame was improved by the addition of a device that automatically laid the next thread for a line of knitting, and by the addition of an extra, thin type of sinker,

A demonstrator working on the framework knitting machine at the Framework Knitters Museum at Ruddington. The machine she is using is a later version of the original Lee frame as it has an automatic adaptation for laying down the yarn for each line of knitting.

that alternated with the earlier ones, to enable finer material to be knitted. With so many moving parts and operations, all the mechanisms had to be held in a stout frame, and as it was mainly intended for use for knitting hosiery, it became known as the stocking frame. The gauge is decided by the number of needles per inch and a half of material, and while the original Lee machine was probably no more than 18-20 gauge, later versions were as high as 40. This meant that, for example, silk stocking could be knitted. At the Ruddington works that will be described shortly, one of the products was tights for ballerinas. By varying the number of needles in use for each row, the stocking could be shaped, so that when it was removed from the frame, the flat fabric could be

sewn into a fully-fashioned stocking. Because the mechanism needed to be worked by both hand and feet, the operative had to sit at the frame and the width was determined by the reach of the arms. This meant that although it was possible to knit two or three identical pieces at one time, that was the limit. The description given here is a simplified version of a complex operation. Working at a stocking frame required skill and a series of complex movements in which hand and foot coordination is an essential.

Lee had the stocking frame completed by 1589. He left the church and set about the essential task of patenting his invention. He presented a pair of stocking to Queen Elizabeth, but she declined to award him a patent. There are two versions of why she declined: one has it that she lost interest on finding he could only make woollen stockings not silk; the other, more flatteringly for the queen, says that she declined because she feared the invention would put too many knitters out of work. Lee did eventually manage to make silk stockings that he sent to the new king James I, but with no more success. He received an indication that he would get a better reception in France, and he and his brother James left England and crossed the Channel. Their hopes for a fortune in France proved as forlorn as they had been in England. William died in France in poverty, and James returned to Britain.

The stocking frame began to come into general use in the seventeenth century, mainly based in London. In 1657, the London knitters received a Charter under Oliver Cromwell, later renewed under Charles II, and became the Worshipful Company of Framework Knitters. The London Guilds had their own pomp and ceremonials, famously having highly decorated barges that took part in processions on the Thames on various official occasions. They were also charitable institutions and, most importantly, were originally intended to provide inviolable rules for the conduct of the trade. They ensured quality was maintained: inspectors were empowered to enter a workshop and cut up any goods that fell below standard and fine the employer. An important clause limited the ratio of qualified journeymen to apprentices. In time, the nature of the Company began to change, with many members having only a slight connection with the trade. The rules on apprenticeship were regularly ignored, and that became a serious problem during the trade recession of the early eighteenth century. These were extremely poor quality, but cheap. Many journeymen were laid off and work was given to boys who had not yet completed their apprenticeship, but the Worshipful Company did nothing about it. The unemployed knitters, having failed to get backing from the authorities who were supposed to regulate the trade took matters into their own hands. Grosvenor Hanson, himself a knitter, wrote a history of the trade in 1831, in which he described what happened to a workshop owned by a Mr. Nicholson. A group of knitters broke into the workshop at night, where they found twelve apprentices working by candlelight. They pushed the boys out and began smashing the frames. The unrest marked the start of a movement out of London and back to the Midlands.

Henson reported that 'so great was the change that no less than eight hundred frames were brought from London to Nottingham, from the year 1732 to 1750 and sold for less than half price; a similar quantity had been removed to Leicester, whilst numbers were laid up as useless or were sold for old iron.' By 1815, when John Blackner wrote his history of Nottingham, the change was complete:

> So much is this town dependent upon the engine, known by the name of the stocking frame, and its appendage machines, that, if it stood still, all other businesses must stand still also. The town may in fact be compared to one vast engine, whose every part is kept in motion by this masterpiece of the mechanic art.

Blackner went on to give a few statistics to show how the trade had changed. In 1641, there were only two frames in the county. In 1739, there were fifty framework knitters, fourteen frame-smiths, twelve needle-makers, eight setters-up and five sink-makers. By the end of the century, there were an estimated 20,000 frames in Nottinghamshire and Leicestershire. Initially, much of the industry relied on knitters working frames in cottages. One can still recognise some of these cottages. Like weavers, knitters required good light and in an age when glass was expensive, most ordinary cottages had small windows. The knitters' cottages were different, though unlike the weavers' cottages, the large windows were on the ground floor. Appropriately, there are good examples in Calverton, where the frame was first developed. Few knitters could afford their own frames, so had to rent them. They brought the raw material from the merchants and were paid by the piece. At first, the pay was good. But increasingly, manufacturers were setting up workshops with many frames, and renting out houses to the workers. A set of workshops can be seen in Ruddington, near Nottingham, which still has many of its original frames and workers' homes.

The beginning of the nineteenth century saw many unscrupulous employers trying to reduce pay by various means. The knitters' pay not only depended on the number of stockings and other items they produced but on the quality. There were many complaints that the rates for higher quality were not being paid as they should have been. A new product appeared, in which material that was woven and then cut into the required shapes was used for stockings. It was cheap and being passed off as knitted though of far inferior quality. The old grievance of employing too many apprentices appeared once again. There was an attempt to use the law to stop the latter practice, using the rules of the old Company. A test case was brought and won – and damages of one shilling awarded, not enough even to cover the cost of bringing the case. A petition to Parliament presented by knitters had no effect on the Members, but did result in the delegates being sacked by their employers when they returned to Nottingham. The knitters now tried to invoke the rules established in the Charter awarded the Company by Charles II that gave them the right to enter workshops and destroy substandard work and ensure apprenticeship laws were obeyed. This gave rise to an outbreak of frame breaking.

The knitters of Nottinghamshire clearly had little faith in the legality of doing so under the protection of the ancient Charter, for the carefully organised raids on targeted workshops were all carried out in the name of a mythical leader, General Ludd. Luddism has now been associated entirely with vain attempts to prevent the introduction of new machinery, especially machinery that would put established craftsmen out of work. This was certainly not the case here; the knitting machines had already been in use for two centuries. It was a last resort. The government that had taken little interest in the plight of the knitters now took immediate action. A Bill was passed through parliament making machine breaking punishable by death. The Luddites published their justification in broadsheets, including this defiant ballad for General Ludd. Here is the first verse.

> Chant no more your old rhymes about bold Robin Hood
> His feats I but little admire
> I will sing the achievements of General Ludd
> Now the hero of Nottinghamshire.
> Brave Ludd was to measure of violence unused
> Till his suffering became so severe
> That at last to defend his own interest he rous'd
> And for the great work did prepare.

They received unlikely support from the aristocratic, but radical, Lord Byron, who argued against the Act that allowed the death penalty for Luddites. He used his maiden speech in the House of Lords to argue against the 1812 machine breaking Bill. He spoke of the work of the police in Nottingham, who, he said, had not been idle: 'Several delinquents have been detained, men liable to conviction on the clearest evidence of poverty; men, who had been nefariously guilty of lawfully begetting several children, whom, thanks to the times, they were unable to nurture.' He also wrote a poem, published in the *Morning Chronicle* in which he condemned the legislators for valuing machines higher then human life. No amount of opposition, however, prevented the Bill being passed and prosecutions followed. In the event, seven Luddites were put on trial. The hearing was moved from Nottingham to Newark to avoid public disturbances: two of the men were acquitted and the others found guilty. The capital punishment was not invoked – instead they were transported for a total of seventy years. The frame breaking subsided as trade improved, but Luddism will appear again in the wool story, but with a different scenario.

The developments of the original frame made it taller and it no longer fitted into most cottage workrooms, so that new machines were housed in specially built workshops. In the 1820s a working complex was set up at Ruddington, near Nottingham. There are two ranges of two-storey workshops, each containing stocking frames. It was also a small community with workers' houses. There was a moderately comfortable house for the manager, but the workers' homes were basic. There was a single downstairs room, which was all-purpose, a bedroom above for parents and an attic for the children. There was a communal washroom for clothes in the yard– only to be used on Mondays – and communal privies. There was also a small chapel, making this a self-contained settlement. When originally set up, there were around 100 working here, but over the years the numbers decreased and it was finally closed in the 1920s. It is now a working museum, where the frames are still regularly used and demonstrated and I spent an afternoon there with Stuart Botterill, while he carefully went through the description of the machine and the methods of working. Seeing the frames in use one can really appreciate the complexity – and it explains why it has been necessary to simplify the description.

In spite of the improvements to the stocking frame, it still produced a flat piece that had to be sewn together to make a stocking. In 1816, Marc Brunel patented a circular knitting machine that worked in much the same way as the Lee original, apart from the needles being arranged in a circle. It was thus able to produce tubes, but as they were the same diameter throughout, they were not really suitable

The workshops at Ruddington.

for making stockings, and the machine found very little use. In 1847, M. Townsend of Nottingham developed another circular machine, this time producing ribbed material and this was followed in 1855, by a circular knitter by A. Paget of Loughborough that was designed to be power driven by means of a belt. The biggest change came with another Townsend invention, the latch needle, in which the latch closed the hook during the knitting process, doing away with the need for pressers, making the whole operation simpler. William Cotton of Loughborough took out a series of patents from1851 to 1863 in which he turned the stocking frame into a power-driven device that could alter the width of the fabric automatically to give shape to the fabric using Jacquard cards. These were first designed in France for the silk industry, and will be discussed in more detail in Chapter Six. Modern knitting machines have all developed from these earlier inventions.

Chapter Four

James Hargreaves and the Spinning Jenny

In the eighteenth century, changes in textile technology were to transform the way in which work was carried out, and the spinning jenny was a vital step in that process. Although it was originally designed specifically for spinning cotton, it would later be developed for wool spinning as well and was a crucial step in the eventual move from the cottage to the factory, so it is worth looking at in some detail.

Very little is known of James Hargreaves' early life. His exact date of birth is uncertain, but he was baptised in Oswaldtwistle in Lancashire on 8 January 1720, and it was usual at that time, because of the high rates of infant mortality, to have the baptism as soon after the birth as possible. He would have had at best a rudimentary education, and he was later described as 'illiterate'. By this period, handloom weaving was one of the major occupations, centred on nearby Blackburn where, when Hargreaves was a teenager, the Livesay brothers were among the major merchants who supplied the raw material to families in the surrounding district. At that time, they were employing 2,400 spinners and 600 weavers. The main cloth was a hybrid, using cotton weft and linen warp. The weavers would have called at the Livesay warehouse to collect the raw material and then returned with the finished cloth to be paid on the basis of the length and quality of the material. Whether the Hargreaves family were actually employed by the Livesays or by another merchant, this would have been the pattern of their working lives.

It was a hard life, with little in the way of comforts. When Oswaldtwistle was assessed for the hearth tax in 1666, there were just two houses with five hearths, and the next largest only had two, while many had just the one. When John Wesley came to preach in this part of Lancashire, he described it as being full of 'wild men' or 'a mob savage as wild beasts'. Their amusements were certainly not gentle; cock fighting and bull baiting were common and there was a particularly brutal sport – kick fighting. This was just what the name suggests, but the men stripped naked apart from iron-tipped wooden clogs. This was the world in which James grew up and into which he took his own place as a weaver. He was described by someone who knew him well in later life as 'a stout, broad-set man, some five feet ten inches high, or rather more'.

The world of weaving was changing. He would have started work as a boy at a time when Kay's flying shuttle was coming into use. The Livesay's had been employing four spinners to supply material for each weaver they employed, but now weaving was speeding up and the demand for more yarn to feed the looms was growing. In 1740, James married Elizabeth Grimshaw and their first child, a daughter, Susan, was baptised in the same church where her father had been baptised in 1744. With a family to support, he would have been glad of any extra source of income. This was true of any weaver at the time, but James Hargreaves, although he lacked any formal education, was obviously an ingenious man. His first idea was not directly connected with the actual process of spinning, but was a way to speed up the essential earlier process of carding. The first improvement had been made in the woollen industry with what were known as stock cards. Instead of a pair of hand cards, vertical wires were attached to one end of a bench. The carder sat on the other end, laid the wool over the spikes and then drew a hand card over them. They were first used in Yorkshire, and by 1808 they were mentioned as having been in use in Lancashire. Hargreaves designed an improved system. Henry Ashworth, a mill owner from the Bolton area, quoted in C. Aspin and S.D. Chapman, *James Hargreaves and the Spinning Jenny,* 1964, described the system.

> [It] consisted in applying two or three cards to the same stock, and suspending the upper cards, which from their weight and size would otherwise have been unmanageable, from the ceiling of the room by a cord passing over a pulley, to the other end of which was affixed a weight or counterpoise.

Ashworth also described meeting an old man who told him of another carding system in use in cottage in Oswaldtwistle, in which the stock was placed vertically and the card moved up and down through a system worked by a foot treadle. There is no evidence to support the idea that this might have been another Hargreaves idea, but it would seem a strange coincidence if two weavers in the area were working on similar ideas at the same time. Hargreaves' improved carding system was probably only used by himself and perhaps a few families in the surrounding area. It can hardly be called an invention, but was simply an improvement on an existing system. The importance of his efforts lies in the fact that he succeeded, which must have encouraged him to think about other ways in which he could improve the supply of thread for the loom.

People tend to like stories that show inventions succeeding thanks to happy accidents – James Watt seeing a kettle boil and inventing the steam engine, for example. Generally, they turn out to have very little if any relation to fact, the Watt story being a classic example as we shall see later. In Hargreaves' case, however, there does seem to be evidence that an accident did indeed play a part in his really important work – the development of the spinning jenny. The story, which was said to be well known in and around Oswaldtwistle, was recorded in Rees's *Cyclopaedia,* generally a reliable source of information. It seems that children were playing in the cottage when one of them knocked over the spinning wheel. The spinner still held the thread in her hand, and the wheel kept spinning in the fallen frame.

> Hargreaves surveyed this with mingled curiosity and attention. He expressed his surprise in exclamations which are still remembered and continued again and again to turn round the wheel as it lay on the floor, with an interest that was at that time mistaken for mere indolence. He had before attempted to spin with two or three spindles affixed to the ordinary wheel, holding the several threads between the fingers of his left hand, but the horizontal position of the spindles rendered this attempt ineffectual; it is therefore not improbable that he derived from the circumstances above-mentioned the first idea of that machine which paved the way for subsequent development.

It certainly seems a logical sequence. One can easily imagine Hargreaves having found a way of using extra cards to speed up one process would then try and work out a way of using more spindles to improve spinning. The jenny itself does, indeed, perform very much as a spinning wheel turned on its side.

Machinery for spinning with several spindles was not a new idea. In 1607, a detailed drawing was published of an Italian device for throwing silk – a similar process to spinning. This consisted of two concentric wooden vertical frames. The inner ring was rotated using power from a water wheel, and laths on the inner frame, rubbed against spindles on the outer, the friction making them turn. The untwisted silk was carried on bobbins above the spindles. From the bobbins, the silk passed through s-shaped wires so that the strands were twisted together. The same technique was used by the

Lombe brothers, who established a silk mill in Derby in the 1720s. A popular story has it that John Lombe had sneaked the plans out of Italy and the furious Italians had their revenge, arranging for him to be poisoned by an assassin. As the machinery was not exactly a secret, details already being widely available, it seems to be just another myth. There was, however, no immediate attempt to develop such a machine for spinning cotton or wool. There was an attempt to develop a water-powered system for spinning cotton, developed by Lewis Paul and John Wyatt in the 1730s, but it never proved very efficient in practice. The field was still open to anyone who could find a practical solution to speeding up the supply of material for weavers, and it was James Hargreaves who had the first real success.

The first jenny was, it seems, quite a simple device. As in the accident, the wheel that would be turned by hand, was laid on its side and was used to turn a number of vertical spindles. The threads were held in a draw bar, a split wooden batten that replaced the spinner's hand. There was an initial problem, not so much with the spinning as winding the spun thread onto bobbins. He made numerous modifications to the original design. It was obvious that if there were going to be many spindles, the clasp would be too heavy to manipulate by holding in the hand and was placed on a frame. The clasp was moved backwards and forwards with one hand, while opening and closing the clasp to grip or release the threads. The other hand was used to turn the wheel. A wire connection was used to control the winding of the finished yarn. In the final version of the jenny, the wheel became vertical instead of horizontal, as can be seen in the illustration on page 72.

The actual operation required a number of separate steps, the unwound threads, the slubbings, were drawn out and the end fastened to the spindles, which were set up at a slight angle to the vertical. The clamp would then be drawn a short distance from the spindles and, shut to hold the threads firmly in place. It would then be pulled back, extending the thread and given a few twists. Once the clamp has been pulled right back, the spinner rapidly turns the wheel and the thread is twisted. The clamp is then moved back and the spun thread wound on to the revolving spindle. It is a complex operation and requires some practice to produce a good, even thread.

This early stage of development comes with several competing accounts, all involving another native of Oswaldtwistle, Robert Peele. He was a near contemporary of Hargreaves but came from a wealthier family. He was originally supposed to be making his living as a farmer, but he joined forces with a local publican William Yates and his brother-in-law Jonathan Howarth to set up in business as a cotton manufacturer and calico printer. At about this time, he dropped the final 'e' from his name on the grounds that as no one pronounced it there was no point in it being there. The Peel family would become famous thanks to his grandson, the politician Sir Robert Peel.

Robert Peel became aware of Hargreaves' experiments and took an interest in them. It is now that everything becomes a little cloudy, as various stories have been told about the relationship. In the first, Peel told the inventor to make his discovery public, or he would do so himself. In the second version, he wanted to keep everything secret so that he could help Hargreaves obtain a patent. Peel's great grandson wrote that Peel provided premises for Hargreaves to work on his machine and helped him with detailed advice. The family even went so far as to suggest that really it was Peel who should have had the credit, but they were all writing long after the event when the participants themselves were all dead. In some accounts, Peel introduced a jenny into his own mill, while in others the only jenny was used by Hargreaves himself to supply material for his own loom. In both accounts, news of the jenny leaked out, and local spinners were determined to smash the machine that threatened their livelihood. What is certain is that Hargreaves' cottage was indeed attacked, probably at some time in 1768, the jenny was destroyed and Hargreaves, in fear of his life, had to hide away, reportedly with the Haworth family, before he could escape and leave Lancashire forever.

The family moved to Nottingham, where demand for yarn to supply the hosiery industry was high. Hargreaves started by supplying jennies to a man called Shipley. It was not long, however, before he met another entrepreneur, Thomas James, who suggested that they went into partnership in a spinning mill, using jennies. James provided the capital by means of a mortgage on another property of his and with that they built a mill at Hockley, now an area close to the centre of the city. Two houses were built alongside the mill, one for each of the two families involved. Hargreaves had hoped to avoid the violence that had driven him from Lancashire, but according to an article in Rees' *Cyclopaedia*, shortly after the mill was opened, Hargreaves and a young woman who had come with him from Lancashire to operate the jenny were attacked. The inventor was wounded and the girl almost died. The jenny, however, was quite quickly accepted, once it became clear that there were real advantages for the spinners. The jenny could be used in a domestic setting just as the spinning wheel had been and in the early days, women spinning with a jenny found they were making more money than ever before. A Parliamentary Report of 1780 recorded that hand spinners in the 1760s had been earning from threepence to fivepence a day while jenny spinners were making at least a shilling a day, over twice as much. That situation did not last. Soon jennies were being installed in mills, some with more than the 24 spindles that were the biggest in use in homes. The women working in the mills found their income halved. In 1779, during a period of depression, there was an outcry against the large jennies and there was a brief outbreak of machine breaking. Some of the more astute mill owners avoided the troubles by sawing off part of the machine to reduce it to an acceptable twenty spindles. The machine breaking was short lived.

The greatest problem originally faced by Hargreaves was pirating of his invention. He took out a patent, but having a patent did not mean that enforcing it was going to be easy. There were jennies built in the Nottingham area, but far more in Lancashire. And the Nottingham jennies soon faced a new threat. Richard Arkwright had devised a new type of spinning machine that used rollers moving at different speeds to draw out the yarn and rotating flyers to impart the twist. Unlike the jenny, everything could be carried out in a continuous set of movements. It no longer needed a human hand to provide the power. His first small mill in Nottingham was literally run on horse power. It was a success, and he soon moved to Cromford in Derbyshire to a far grander mill in which everything was worked by a water wheel – hence the name of water frame for his spinning machine. The Hargreaves mill was still using jennies with just 16 spindles each – though in Lancashire far bigger machines were already in use. The hosiers were now buying their cotton from Arkwright and his associates: Hargreaves could not compete. He and James took the obvious step: out went the jennies and they installed water frames under licence. The jennies were put up for sale, not in Nottingham, but in Manchester, in 1777, where the advert offered up three carding engines worked by horses and fifty jennies, each of 16 spindles. There is no record of whether they were bought or not. It was to be one of the last acts of Hargreaves' life. He died in April 1778, not a rich man, but far more comfortably off than he would have been had he not had an inventive mind. James bought out his share of the joint business from his widow for £400, equivalent to around £80,000 today.

That is by no means the end of the jenny story. Improvements had been made, including changing the original horizontal

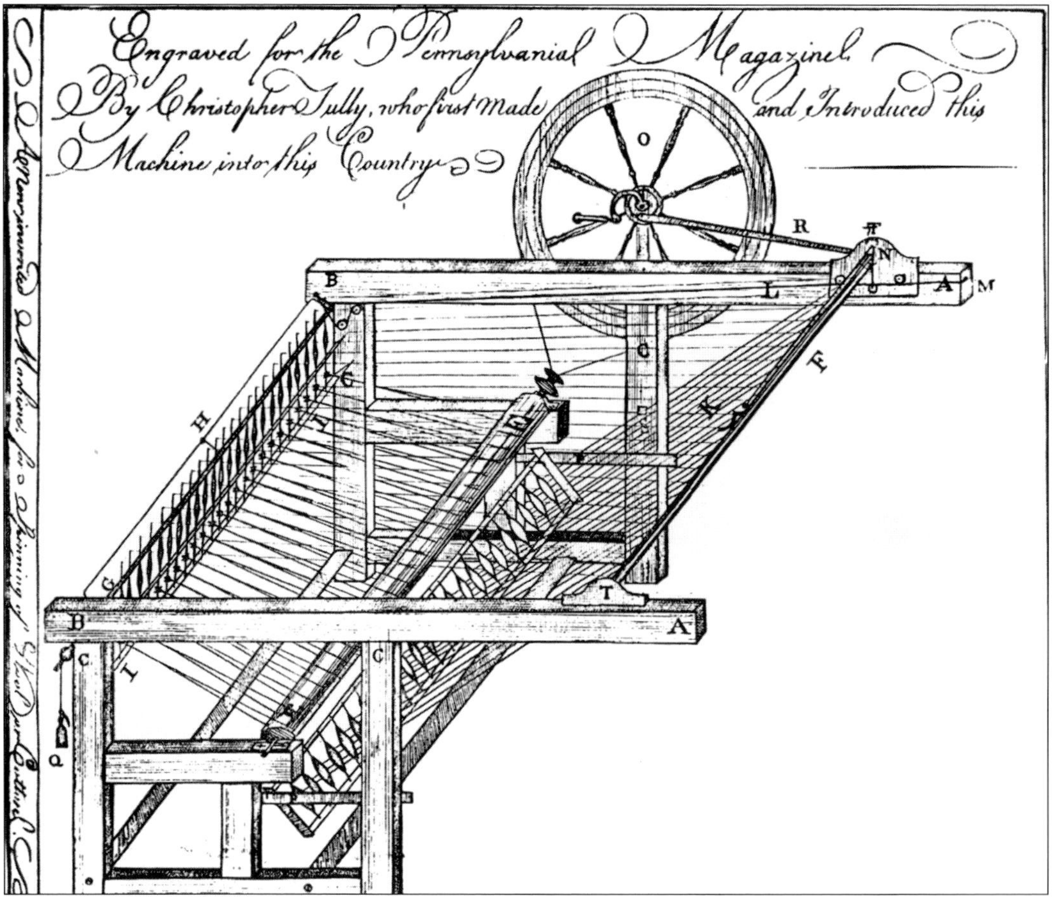

One of the first spinning jennies to be imported into America. It is slightly different from Hargeaves' original in that the wheel at the side is vertical instead of horizontal.

wheel for a vertical one. The early jennies had been too small to use for spinning wool, but as the larger versions became available, they started to be taken up by Yorkshire manufacturers. According to W.B. Crump and Gertrude Chorbal in their *History of the Huddersfield Woollen Industry*, 1935, the 18-spindle jenny was a great success; 'every clothier (or manufacturer) had one or more in his house, and also kept a number of women spinning yarn for him in their cottages. So began the manufacturer's "warehouse" in the upland hamlets.' Much of the work went, as it had done for generations, to workers in cottages, but one man introduced a fundamental change. Benjamin Gott was born at Calverley near Leeds in 1762. His father was a highly successful civil engineer and was wealthy enough to get his son an apprenticeship to the most important cloth merchants in Leeds, Wormald and Fountaine, and then buy him a partnership. He recognised that the textile world was changing and in 1792 he bought a plot of land beside the River Aire, known as Bean Inge, where he built a woollen mill and installed an estimated forty to fifty jennies. This was an integrated mill, used for both spinning and weaving, and Gott installed all the latest equipment, including a Boulton & Watt steam engine. The mill was a huge success and the outbreak of war with France, far from affecting his business, brought him fresh trade, supplying blankets and cloth for uniforms. By 1800, he was employing 1,000 workers and even then they could not keep up with demand. He built a second mill in Leeds, Armley Mills, now home to the Leeds Industrial Museum. He made a fortune and was able to live in grand style in a mansion, Armley House, set in parkland designed by the famous landscape gardener Humphrey Repton. Gott and the jenny began a revolution in wool manufacturing in Leeds. Other Yorkshire mills introduced jennies and one factory at Hebble, near Halifax, had thirteen 60-spindle jennies, five 50-spindle, thee 48-spindle and thirty-six 40-spindle. That's a grand total of 2,614 whirling spindles in the one mill, doing the work that would have required over 2,000 spinners working on the old hand spinning wheels.

All the main woollen cloth areas of Britain had jennies at one time, and in Wales they continued in regular use right through to the early years of the twentieth century. Jennies were sold abroad to many countries, but nowhere was their arrival to have a more dramatic effect than in America. A jenny was exhibited in Philadelphia in 1775, the year that the War of Independence started. Britain had always regarded America as a producer of raw materials, notably cotton, and as a market for manufactured goods, and to keep the status quo, laws were passed forbidding the establishment of cloth manufacture in America. Such restrictive laws were inevitably very unpopular and were among the factors that caused the colonial Americans to fight for independence. Europeans had by then introduced sheep to the continent and the way was open after the war to start manufacturing. John Shaw, with John and Arthur Schofield, left Saddleworth in Yorkshire and settled in Massachusetts, where they made a modest start in business with one 40-spindle jenny and a single handloom at Charlestown. When that succeeded, they moved on to build a small woollen mill at Byfield, 30 miles from Boston. It was modest success but was the start of the American woollen industry in New England. It was in this area that the biggest jenny ever built with 150 spindles was set to work at Uxbridge in 1824. The American wool industry never achieved the importance of cotton, but it did make a substantial contribution to the economy of the young country, and the jenny was there at the start. It was to be the last invention of the industry to be hand powered. The next generation of machines would depend on the water wheel and the steam engine to keep them turning. In their day, however, the jennies formed a vital link in the progression from home working to the factory.

Chapter Five

Samuel Crompton and the Mule

If the jenny was important to the wool industry, even though originally developed for cotton, that is even more true of the mule. Even today, there are working woollen mills in Britain, where mules are still in use.

Samuel Crompton's family had been farmers at Tonge, near Bolton, but by his grandfather's time they were, like many others, adding weaving as an extra source of income. The combination was not a success, and shortly before Samuel's birth in December 1753, his father George Crompton sold the farm. He stayed on as a tenant, but then left for a smaller house and abandoned farming. In 1758, they all moved again, this time to the old manor house at Tonge, Hall i' th' wood. This elaborate wooden-framed Tudor building looks remarkably grand, and would have done so in Crompton's time, but they were not occupying the whole building. It had been split up into smaller units, so the family only occupied a part of it. Unfortunately, there is now no way of being sure which parts they lived in. The house, however, has been fully restored and contains many items relating to Crompton and his work.

Shortly after their arrival at the manor, George Crompton died, but his widow Betty stayed on and in 1764, she was granted a lease on the property, together with around five acres of land, at a rent of £9 18s per annum. There was a curious clause in the agreement that required her to keep one beagle and a fighting-cock for the owner or pay a penalty of £1 a year. She was able to keep a few cows on the land and earned money by spinning on a Saxony wheel, with the help

Hall i' th' Wood, Bolton, the home of Samuel Crompton in which he built his spinning mule. The illustration by Selim Rothwell shows the house c.1840.

of her children, Samuel and his two sisters, weaving fustian, a heavy cotton and linen cloth.

Samuel went to school at Little Bolton. His stay there was brief, but he was able to continue his education by going to evening classes until he was sixteen. His surviving letters show him to be a literate and stylish writer and he had inherited his father's love of music. He made a violin for himself and added to the family income by playing with the orchestra at a little theatre in Great Bolton, being paid eightpence a performance, round about £6 at today's prices – not much, but it all helped the family survive.

We know something of his early life from his own letters to Sir Joseph Banks, the eminent scientist and President of the Royal Society. He wrote, 'As soon as I was able, a daily task was assigned to me to spin.' At the age of just ten, he was sent to learn to weave for a year, and soon after was able to work as a weaver. It seems that the family were able to turn their hands to anything in the textile world, and in 1769 one of the new jennies was installed at Hall i' th' wood. It was a small machine with just eight spindles. This was used to supply the cotton weft for the fustian, but the old Saxony wheel was still used for the linen warp threads. The industry was changing, and here was an increasing demand for lighter, all cotton garments. It was now that Samuel began attempts to produce suitable warp threads on the jenny. He found great difficulty in producing threads of even quality. In spite of the widespread use of the jenny, he declared that only one in ten of the yarns produced was actually of good quality. He was convinced that if a machine could make one good yarn, there was no reason why a machine shouldn't be able to make all the yarns good. He began to work at the problem in 1774.

It seems that much of the old manor was empty, so, as he wrote:

> … there was a number of spare rooms, any of which I could take to my own private use, no one knowing what I was about, and here the whole of my powers both of body and mind were concentrated into one continued endeavour to accomplish the object of my pursuit, which was that every thread should be (as near as possible) equally good.

He was aware, as anyone in the textile industry at the time would have been, that new machines were not always welcomed and even when they were introduced, secrecy was essential to prevent the idea being pirated. He mainly worked by night at the invention, and locals who saw candles flickering in the ancient building simply assumed it was haunted. Fortunately, no one considered that the young weaver was working on an invention that might put some of them out of work.

In fact, it was to take him five years to come up with his first attempt, which had, he later wrote, cost him 'every shilling I had in the world'. It was a period of unrest. The country was at war with France, trade was poor and it was certainly not a good time to introduce a new labour-saving machine to the world, especially in Lancashire. Richard Arkwright had deliberately chosen Cromford for his water-frame, well away from any potential problems with dissatisfied cottage spinners. His machine, developed in 1768, used rollers moving at different speeds to draw out the cotton and a rotating flyer to provide twist. It was powered by water wheel, and, unlike the jenny, could never be applied to home use. But by now he had boldly advanced into Lancashire, and his machinery had been installed in a mill at Chorley. In October 1779, thousands of Lancashire workers descended on the mill, which was guarded by just fifty soldiers. There was no hope of defending against such a number and everything in the mill was destroyed. According to a letter written by Josiah Wedgwood, who happened to be in Lancashire at the time:

> On Tuesday morning we heard their drum at about two miles distant from Bolton, a little before we left the place, and their professed design was to take Bolton, Manchester and Stockport in their way to Cromford, and to destroy all the engines, not only in these places, but throughout all England.

Crompton would have heard those same drums and seen the men gathering. He took his machine to pieces and hid them away.

Once the rioting had calmed down, he reassembled his prototype and began using it for spinning. The first version was really little more than an improved jenny, which is what he was hoping to produce. The clasp was replaced by a pair of rollers held together by springs. The biggest difference was that now, instead of moving the clasping rollers away from the spindles to stretch the yarn, he mounted the spindles on a carriage running on rails and pulled them away from the rollers. This gave greater control and he was able to contain the slubbings on a stationary frame. He was able to produce finer thread than he had been doing on the jenny, but he had not yet produced a wholly new machine. The next development was crucial. He added a second pair of rollers behind the original and using a pulley system made the front pair run faster than the back. This was, of course, an idea already developed by Arkwright to pull out the yarn. So, his new machine used ideas derived from both the jenny and the water frame: it was a hybrid, hence the name by which it came to be known – the spinning mule.

Originally, Crompton had been spinning for his own use as a weaver, but 'finding by experience that when I stopped spinning to weave what I had spun that my machine by stopping did not do as well as when kept constant working it determined me to concentrate on spinning altogether, knowing that my yarn would answer for every purpose of the trade.' He had achieved his ambition of producing fine, consistent yarn. The fineness of the yarn is given in 'counts' – a number given the length of thread needed to produce a given weight. In current metric units, for example, a 60 count would mean 60,000 metres of yarn would weigh one kilogram, 80 count, 80,000 and so on. In Crompton's time Imperial units would have been used, but the principle is the same – the higher the count, the finer the thread. Crompton was able to get good prices. According to Thomas Midgley's pamphlet *The Spinning Mule*, 1927, he was selling 60s at 25 shillings a pound and 80s at 42 shillings, some of the latter going to Samuel Oldknow for manufacturing fine muslin. This seems extraordinary as Oldknow, one of the most successful manufacturers of the day, was also spinning yarn, though not of that quality. Even so, the yarn he was selling only fetched a fraction of those prices. His account books for December 1792 show him as having sold 1,000lb of yarn for a total of £181 16s 9d, or around 4s a pound. The discrepancy seems just too great: something seems to be amiss. Whether the quoted figures are accurate or not, Crompton was prospering, and was doing well enough to get married in 1780. His wife Mary – her surname seems to have been either Pimlott or Pimley – had been working as a jenny spinner. They moved into a cottage next to the Hall. The following year they had a son George and a year after that another boy, Samuel. At this point they moved to Sharples, not far from Hall i' th' wood.

Although he had moved out of his old home, he still had his workroom there, where he continued to spin. His success brought more attention that he would have ever wanted, being a somewhat modest man. Everyone it seemed wanted the new yarn – and everyone wanted the secret as to how it was produced. It has been said that even Arkwright made the trip to Bolton to find out about the new machine. Hall i' th' wood became a house under siege – there was a rumour that while most merely tried to peer through the windows to find out what was going on, one enterprising individual managed to get into the loft and bored a hole in the ceiling of the workroom to get a glimpse of the new machine. 'It was', Crompton wrote, 'like a lighted match to gunpowder – everyone looking on me as a prodige'.

Crompton was, like many inventors, rather more adept at mechanics than business. It was obvious that he was not going to be able to keep his machine secret, and invited a Bolton merchant John Pilkington to advise him. He could not afford to apply for a patent and, even if he had been able to do so, he would almost certainly have been challenged by Richard Arkwright, who would claim that the use of rollers had been copied from his water frame. Pilkington suggested that he should exhibit the machine at the Manchester Royal Exchange, the centre for merchants dealing in cotton that had been established in 1721. A subscription would then be opened, and manufacturers would contribute as recognition of the inventor making his work widely available. It was expected to raise £200, but in the event all he got was £72 11s 6d.

The Crompton family moved into Bolton in 1790, where it appears that he used the mule to make rovings, the aligned fibres that will be fed to the spinning machine for twisting to make the actual yarn, rather than yarn. In his spare time, he was an active member of the Swedenborgian Chapel, based on the teachings of the Swedish theologian. With the help of his son, he built a small organ in his own house and the chapel choir would come round to practice, often singing hymns written by Crompton himself. The family were never very well off and in 1796 there was a personal tragedy with the loss of his wife. The situation in the cotton industry had changed in the meantime. Arkwright's patent had been overthrown by the courts and, in theory, there was now nothing to prevent Crompton applying for a patent. But it was too late – the mule was now too widely used for a patent to be effective. However, help was at hand.

John Kennedy was a Scot, who had moved to Manchester where he formed a partnership with James McConnell, initially manufacturing spinning machinery, including jennies. They then abandoned that side of the business and turned to spinning, eventually building three imposing mills in the Ancoats area of the town, making them one of the leading manufacturers of the time. He started a fund to raise money to compensate Crompton for his work in making the mule generally available, and between 1803 and 1807, £444 was handed over. With the funds, Crompton was able to rent the top floor of a factory in Back King Street, Bolton, where he installed his mules and worked with his sons. He continued to struggle financially, largely due to his own natural modesty, an admirable quality, but not one that helps in aggressive salesmanship. There were various attempts to raise money for the inventor of the mule that was being used throughout Lancashire at the time with no reward for its inventor. It was at this time that he wrote to Sir Jospeh Banks for help and advice. An appeal was made to parliament in 1812 and it seemed that a committee was likely to approve a payment, but on the day they were due to meet, the prime minister Spencer Perceval was assassinated, and all parliamentary business was put on hold. A story circulated that an award of as much as £20,000 was about to be recommended by Perceval, but no one has ever found any actual evidence to support that claim. Eventually, parliament recommended a payment of £5,000. To put that in context, the other inventor of spinning machinery Arkwright, left an estate worth £500,000 at his death in 1792. £5,000 sems a meagre reward for a man whose invention was now being used throughout the cotton industry. Crompton died in 1826 and by that time his mule had become a vital part of the textile industry. Shortly afterwards, it was be improved again, with changes that would make it even more valuable. In 1830, Richard Roberts made the mule self-acting, in other words all parts of the machine and every action could be powered by a single source, such as a water wheel. Its use was by then not confined to the cotton industry, but proved invaluable to the woollen industry as well. It was not the only device in use. The jenny had proved unsuitable for spinning the fine worsted yarn. Arkwright investigated using a version of his water frame, the throstle, by moving the rollers further apart to take the worsted fibres that were much longer than the cotton for which the original has been designed.

Mules continue to be used in woollen mills right up to the present time. I recently visited Trefriw woollen mill in North Wales, where the present mules have been in use for over sixty years. These mules, though not the biggest ever made, are still impressive, with 360 spindles. I have always found watching mule spinning to be absolutely fascinating – the steady movement of the carriage to and fro, the whirling

The mule was later made self-acting, as seen here at the C.W.S. Mill at Batley, Yorkshire in 1913.

spindles and the twisting threads – everything so perfectly co-ordinated. With this many spindles, thread breakages are inevitable. So, the operative has to walk backwards and forwards with the mechanism, keeping an eye on the threads and rejoining any that have broken. One woman I spoke to at a woollen mill said she had no need to go the gym, as she had worked out that she walked backwards and forwards for seven miles every day. Once the bobbins were full of yarn, the machine had to be stopped and the doffers moved in – there were 360 full bobbins to remove to be replaced by 360 empty ones to be connected up with threads, before the whole operation could restart. Although it was originally developed for the cotton industry, the importance of the mule to the

Repairing a broken thread on a mule.

woollen industry cannot be overestimated. Crompton knew he had achieved something very special. His tragedy was that he never received either the recognition or the reward he deserved. Our next inventor had a very different life story to tell.

There was a further development of the jenny and the mule that appeared shortly afterwards, the slubbing billy. The rotating spindles were set on a wheeled frame, running on rails, but the carded wool was first passed through the billy rollers to slightly condense it. The aim was not to produce yarn, but lightly twisted wool, slubbings, that will later be passed to the mule to give the final twist. The last surviving slubbing billy can be seen in the woollen mill on Islay.

Chapter Six

Cartwright and the Power Loom

Apart from the Rev. William Lee, all the inventions that affected the woollen industry had come from men who worked as weavers and spinners. There had been several attempts to produce a loom in which all the mechanisms could be worked by an external power source, such as a water wheel, but none had proved really successful. It was another clergyman who was to succeed, but he was in a very different social class from Rev. Lee.

Edmund Cartwright was born into a wealthy and land-owning family in Marnham, Nottinghamshire in 1743. From school, he went to University College, Oxford, graduated and was elected a Fellow of Magdalene College. After Oxford he was ordained in the Church of England and was appointed to the living at Brampton and then at Goadby-Marwood in Leicestershire. Like many eighteenth-century vicars, he never devoted all his time to the church and his congregation. He had literary aspirations and wrote several poems that were published anonymously, before producing an epic poem in two parts: *Armine and Elvira*. It was popular at the time but is now difficult to find a mention anywhere – it is in no modern anthologies nor do any quotes appear in dictionaries of quotations. Looking at it today, one can see why it has vanished from library shelves. Here are the first two verses, splattered with capital letters.

A Hermit on the Banks of Trent
Far from the World's bewildering Maze
To humble scenes of calm Content
Has fled from brighter, busier days.

Portrait of Edmund Cartwright by Robert Fulton.

If haply from his guarded Breast
Should steal the unsuspected Sigh
And Memory, an unbidden Guest
And former Passions fill'd his Eye.

He went on to write more poems and regularly contributed to literary reviews. Given this background, it is all the more remarkable that he should ever have become involved in inventing a machine for an industry with which he had no connection whatsoever.

It appears that he had gone on a visit to the popular Derbyshire spa of Matlock in the summer of 1784, where he met a group of men from Manchester, all involved in the cotton industry. They invited him to join them in visiting Arkwright's nearby cotton mill. Cartwright was suitably impressed but wondered why spinning had been mechanised but not weaving. The Manchester men were adamant that given the complexity of the loom, this would be impossible. Apparently, Cartwright up to this point had never really looked at a loom – if he had been more familiar with its workings he might have agreed. Instead, he regarded this is an interesting intellectual challenge. He decided to design a power loom.

His first attempt was a curious device. Power was supplied by two men, who had to give up after an hour, totally exhausted. He described it himself: 'The warp was placed perpendicularly, the reed fell with the weight of at least half a hundredweight, and the springs which threw the shuttle were strong enough to have thrown a Congreve rocket.' As a 32lb Congreve artillery rocket had a range of some 2,000 yards, this was certainly a lot of power. But it was definitely not a practical power loom. At this stage, Cartwright did what he perhaps should have done at the start and began studying the actual workings of a handloom. He set about working on a system where levers and cams would do the work previously done by the weaver's hands and feet. He took out three patents, between 1786 and 1788. Cams worked by levers pressed on the treadles to replace the feet. To move the picker, a cam pressed down on a spring, then once the pressure was released it would jerk open and an attachment would send the shuttle on its way.

There were two problems that the loom did not overcome. If the weft broke or the shuttle stuck, then the machinery would simply continue uselessly running. That meant someone had to be constantly minding it – and if the loom still needed a single operative, manufacturers had no incentive to invest in a machine that provided no saving in labour costs. Cartwright solved those problems with an automatic device to stop the loom if the weft failed, and another that also stopped it if the shuttle was not in the box for the picker to hit. Having spent a great deal of time and money on his invention, it was now time to try and profit from it.

Cartwright attempted to interest Manchester businessmen in his invention with little success, so he decided to make use of it himself. He moved to the woollen manufacturing area of Yorkshire, setting up his looms in a spinning and weaving mill in Doncaster. This was successful and he moved to an even larger, four-storey water-powered mill in the town, with twenty looms. As other manufacturers of the time had done, he began employing children to attend the looms. Not every visitor was impressed, and when his friend the poet George Crabbe visited the mill with his wife, the lady was horrified by the experience; 'When she entered the building, full of engines thundering with relentless power, yet under the apparent management of children, the bare idea of the inevitable hazards attendant on such stupendous undertakings quite overcame her feelings and she burst into tears.' The effect on anyone not used to this world of powered machinery would in any case have been dramatic since, as anyone who has ever been in a room full of power looms will know, the noise is literally deafening. The mill was a financial disaster, but not it seems because the new looms failed to work. The likeliest explanation is that, like so many inventors before him, Cartwright was a bad businessman.

Cartwright did manage to get an order from a Manchester manufacturer for what has been reported as somewhere between 400 and 500 looms. When set to work, one operative was able to look after two looms. Just a few had been delivered and set to work, however, when the mill mysteriously caught fire and everything was destroyed. Inevitably, given the earlier outbreaks of machine breaking when those machines seemed to

Power loom in the weaving shed at Ham Mill, Stroud, 1928. Each loom is powered by a belt from the overhead line shafting.

threaten the livelihood of existing workers, arson was suspected but never proved. There was no rush from others to take up the invention. Cartwright never made the fortune he had hoped for from his power loom, but he did receive a grant of £10,000 from the government in recognition of his work – twice that awarded to the equally inventive and unfortunate Hargreaves. He used the money to buy a farm at Battle in Kent, where he died in 1823.

There were to be many improvements to the power loom over the years. One notable improvement was made by William Horrocks of Stockport. His loom of 1803 used a crank to move the slay, the moveable arm holding the reeds. Where earlier looms such as Cartwright's had been largely constructed of wood, the Horrocks version had a sturdy iron frame. The loom was fine for making plain cloth, or one with a simple pattern, such as a stripe. Creating more complex patterns created a different problem. The early power looms replicated the action of the handloom, in which the headles were generally moved by just two treadles. The weft would produce a single colour, unless the shuttle was removed and replaced by one holding a different coloured thread. The latter problem had been largely solved even before the power loom came into use, by the use of drop boxes, each box holding a different shuttle that could be dropped into place. By far the most effective method of creating a pattern by the selective raising and lowering of headles was developed in France for the silk industry.

To create intricate patterns, silk weavers used a draw boy, who squatted on top of the loom and using a given pattern, pulled up the appropriate headles for each pass of the shuttle. In 1745, Jacques de Vaucanson developed a system to control the headles

A drop shuttle loom at the C.W.S. Mill, Batley: the individual shuttles can be seen on the left hand side of the loom.

using punched cards, but it still required two human operatives. The big change came when Joseph Marie Jacquard developed the idea to make it automatic. This was a device that sat on top of the loom. The cards were sewn together and at each pass a different card appeared above the headles. When the loom mechanism activated the headles, lifting them up, they either passed through one of the holes or were stopped by hitting the card. It has often been referred to as the world's first working computer system – and the early computers were also fed by punched cards or tape. The Jacquard looms could produce very intricate patterns and were particularly useful in the carpet industry.

The power loom was not Cartwright's only contribution to the woollen industry. He also devised a machine for combing wool, which up to then was still carried out by hand. The conditions under which the hand combers had worked were wretched. Dr Thackrah investigated working conditions in the nineteenth century, publishing his results in *Effects of Arts, Trades and Manufactures on Health and Longevity* in 1831. Here is what he had to say about combers.

> Wool-combers work in apartments which, from the fire employed to heat the combs, are kept at the temperature of 80. The fires are made of charcoal. A light dust arises from the wool. The lungs suffer so much that many persons cannot pursue the employment. The men, however, whom we found in the rooms appeared quite healthy, and we were informed that out of one hundred individuals only two or three were absent from illness.

The combers had, according to an anonymous pamphlet of 1741, formed a 'combination' paying twopence or threepence a week into a fund for the sick. It was also a combination that attempted to operate a closed shop, insisting that only men who joined the club could be employed, and anyone employing large numbers from outside the combination

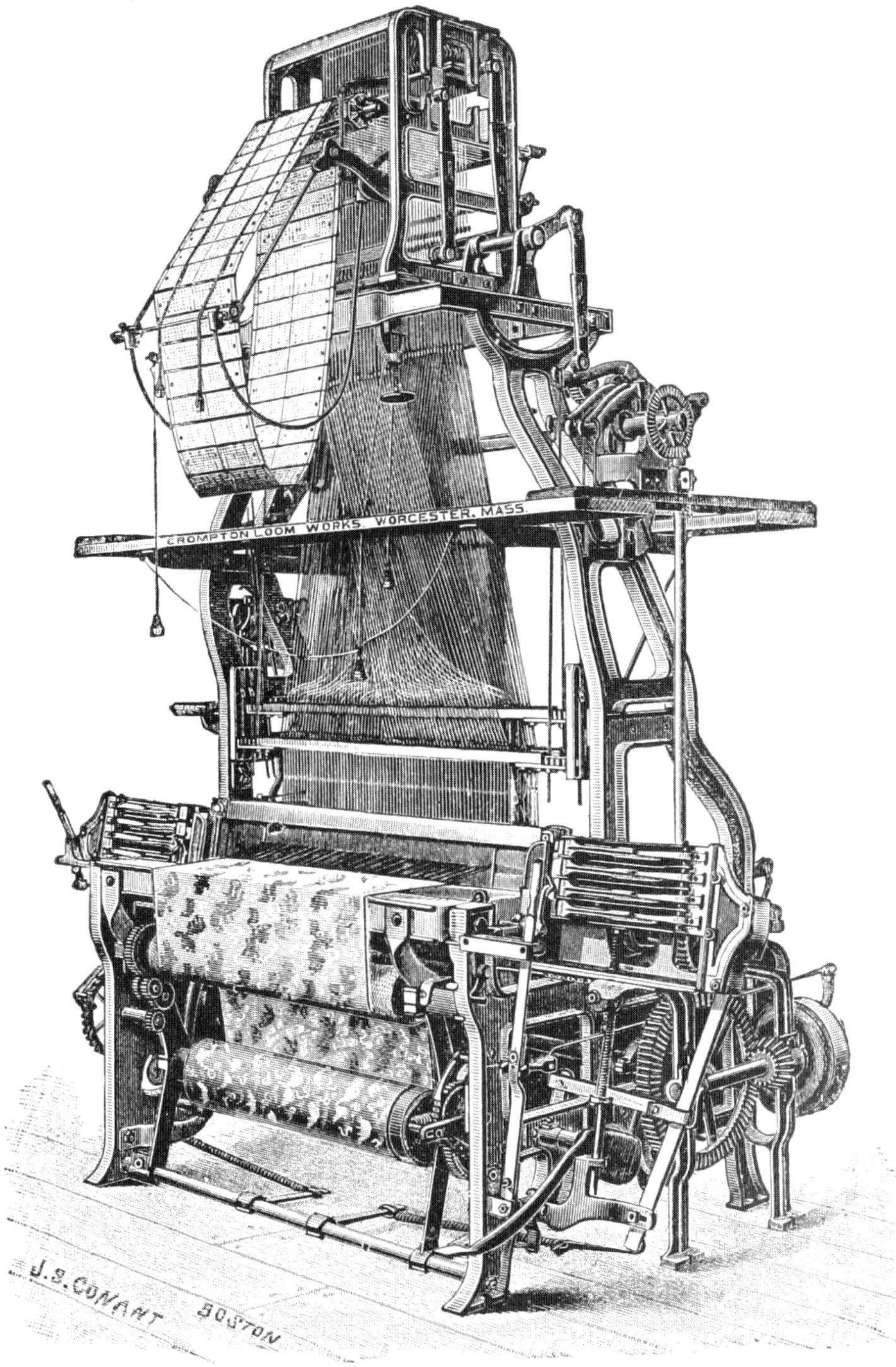

A jacquard loom being used for weaving patterned carpet, from *Popular Science Monthly*, 1891.

would be faced by a strike and 'often times they were not satisfied with that, but would abuse the honest man that would labour, and in riotous manner beat him, break his comb pots, and destroy his working tools'. As can be imagined, they did not welcome the introduction of the new machines, but did not resort to breaking them in protest.

Crompton's combing machine that he patented in 1792 consisted of a circular, rotating frame roughly five to six feet in diameter, set with the teeth of the comb on the inside of the rim and pointing towards the centre. Above that was a grooved roller onto which the wool was placed and was then lowered onto the frame, to lash on the wool. As the wheel rotated, long fibres were removed by a set of rollers and the shorter by combs. The combs were heated by a stove under the frame. Because it was said to do the work of twenty men, it was known as 'Big Ben', which was apparently the nickname of a successful prize fighter. Several improved combing machines were introduced over the years. One of these, patented by J. Platt in 1827, was described by the enthusiastic advocate of new machinery, Andrew Ure, in his book *The Philosophy of Manufacture* in 1855. This version had two comb wheels.

> Large machines are now at work in Leeds. In one of them, the comb-wheels are ten feet in diameter and are furnished with hollow spikes filled with steam which keeps the whole apparatus at a proper combing heat. These wheels are made to revolve slowly while a boy, seated on the ground, dresses one of them with wool. They are then made to revolve with great rapidity ... during which revolutions they gradually approach each other.

There were further improvements over the years. Having briefly had an excursion back to the start of the whole cloth-making process, in the next chapter the emphasis is back to the final stages.

Chapter Seven

Cloth Dressing

Cloth dressing had already been partially mechanised with the introduction of gig mills to raise the nap. The next stage was cropping, cutting the nap with heavy shears, which remained the work of skilled craftsmen right through to the early years of the nineteenth century. The croppers were the elite of the workforce, a fact reflected in their pay. One of the most prosperous areas for cloth making was the Colne valley that spread westward from Huddersfield to Marsden, a small mill town at the end of the valley, before the land rears up to Standedge Fell that divides Yorkshire from Lancashire. It was in Marsden that two former blacksmiths, the brothers Enoch and James Taylor began making finishing-frames that used rotary cutters to crop the nap. This was at a time when Britain was deeply engaged in the Napoleonic Wars, trade was bad and work scarce. It was not a good time to introduce machines that were said to be able to do the work of ten croppers. The croppers reacted with a prolonged period of machine breaking, organised as the Nottingham knitters had been under the banner of Ned Ludd. They used heavy hammers that they called 'Enochs' – the slogan was 'Enoch made 'em and Enoch'll break 'em'. The name lived on in the Colne Valley. When I visited the Sair Inn in Slaithwaite some years ago, they were selling a headache-inducing strong ale called 'Enoch's Hammer'.

The Taylors sold frames to John Horsfall of Ottiwell's Mill, close to their smithy. Paradoxically, the Luddites seem not to have had any animosity to Enoch Taylor himself, but all their anger was directed against the mill owners, who were installing the machines. Horsfall was one of the most hated, not only because he installed the frames, but he was also a loud advocate for them, trying to persuade other local mill owners to follow his example. He was a belligerent man, who is said to have declared he would fill his mill with the machines 'if he had to ride up to his saddle girths in Luddite blood'. The story of how the machine breakers were organised appears in John Cowgill, *An Historical Account of the Luddites*, 1862.

The main organiser in the Huddersfield area was a local cropper, George Mellor. The Luddites had committees that met in secret, and members paid a small weekly contribution, specifically intended to provide help for the families of any members unlucky enough to be caught and jailed. When they set out on machine-breaking nights, no names were ever used – everyone was given a number – and many went in disguise. The Luddites had a blood-curdling oath, that included details of what would happen to anyone who betrayed a fellow member. He agreed that his punishment was to be:

> … sent out of the world by the next brother who shall meet me, and my name and character blotted out of existence, and never to be remembered but with contempt and abhorrence: and I further now do swear, that I will use my best endeavours to punish by death any traitor or traitors, should any rise up among us

Parliament reacted by passing legislation that made taking the oath punishable by death.

At first, the Luddites simply sent anonymous letters to mill owners, threatening to smash the machines, at which point a few simply removed the machines. Others flatly refused and the machine breaking began, but some mill owners set up defences in the mills that seemed to make attack impossible. The two leading manufacturers in defending their property were Horsfall and William Cartwright who owned Rawfolds

Mill at Liversedge, a few miles south of Bradford. A coin was tossed by the Luddites to decide which should be attacked first, and it fell to Cartwright. On the night of 11 April 1812, an eyewitness estimated that about 100 men were mustered for the attack. The whole affair was conducted like a military operation, with two bodies of men with muskets, lined up in two rows of ten, followed by a line of men with pistols and the rest carried various items such as sticks and axes to carry out the destruction and break into the mill. They knew that there was an alarm bell at the mill, which if rung would have brought in a detachment of cavalry, so the first order given was to fire at the bell and put it out of action.

Cartwright had been sleeping in the mill for some time, and had with him five soldiers, four mill workers and a supply of muskets and ammunition. A guard dog gave the alarm, shortly after midnight. An attempt to ring the bell failed when the rope broke, but at once the Luddites began firing at the mill and attempting to break down the door, while the men within the mill returned fire through loopholes in the wall. Cartwright gave his own description of what happened that night.

> The firing was kept up regularly by the people out of doors for a considerable time. I continued to hear the most violent crashing and hammering against the doors, and occasionally heard cries of 'Bang up. In with you' 'Are you in' 'Keep close' … I distinctly heard the expressions 'In with you lads'. 'D them, kill them every one'. A constant firing on both sides continued for some time, how long I could not state exactly, but from the number of shots fired by us I suppose it must have been about twenty minutes. After the firing from without had slackened, we abated ours within, with a view to saving the effusion of blood. I then heard a confused alarm on one side, as if an attempt was making to carry off the wounded men. After the firing had ceased I heard the cries of the wounded men.

***Above*: Lavenham Church,** Norfolk largely built in the fourteenth century, financed by local wool merchants and regarded as one of the grandest of all the wool churches.

***Right*: An ornate** Incan wool tunic.

Spinning on the great wheel from George Walker's book *The Costume of Yorkshire*, 1814.

The Mixed-Cloth Hall in Leeds, built between 1756 and 1758.

Yorkshire knitters were famous for their speed. This illustration is another from *The Costume of Yorkshire*.

A nineteenth century book of knitting patterns.

***Left*: A contemporary** print of General Ludd leading the Yorkshire machine breakers.

***Below*: Weaving Donegal** tweed at the Triona Donegal Tweed Centre.

***Above*: Saltaire provides** a contrast with the scene from Huddersfield. Sir Titus Salt provided a park next to the mill and well-built houses for his employees.

***Right*: The elegant** interior of Stanley Mill, King's Stanley: the mill closed recently.

***Left*: A replica** of the Pazyryk rug: the original is in the Hermitage Museum, St. Petersburg.

***Below*: The Ardabil** carpet, now in the Victoria and Albert Museum, London.

Hand weaving a carpet in a Turkish factory.

The former Templeton carpet factory on Glasgow Green is said to have been inspired by the Doge's Palace in Venice.

***Above*: Gobelins tapestry** in the Tapestry Room at Croome Court, Worcestershire.

***Left*: The Graham** Sutherland tapestry in Coventry Cathedral.

It turned out that several had been wounded and one young man died a few days later. The attack on the mill had failed, no frames had been smashed and one of their company had died. George Mellor realised that an attack on the Horsfall mill would be likely to have a similarly disastrous end, as it would now be even more heavily defended. Instead, he decided not to attack the mill, but to turn his attention on the owner. William Horsfall had always bragged about being unafraid of anything the Luddites might do, so he rode back to Marsden from Huddersfield market alone as he did every week. On 28 April, Mellor, together with Thomas Smith, Benjamin Walker and William Thorpe were armed and waiting for him. He was shot three times and died of his injuries.

The hunt for the murderers began, but the Luddite oath bound everyone in silence, until the authorities offered a £2,000 reward for information. That was a fortune, far more than any cropper could expect to earn after a lifetime's work. The temptation was too great for Benjamin Walker; he turned King's evidence – which freed him from prosecution – and claimed the reward. The other three involved were found guilty and hanged. As a result of evidence also given about the attack on the mill, more men were arrested and another seventeen publicly hanged and seven more transported. It effectively marked the end of resistance to the new machines. In Yorkshire.

When cloth cutting machinery was introduced into the West of England, there was no similar uprising. One example is preserved in the Stroudwater Textile Trust museum at Dunkirk Mill, Nailsworth. This is a cross cutter, in which the actual cropping is done by a rotating cylinder with attached cutting blades, that was moved across the cloth stretched over a table. It would have been worked by either water or steam power. Machines such as this attracted the attention of a man from nearby Stroud, Edwin Budding. He realised that if you made a smaller version of the cutting cylinder, mounted it

A close-up view of the blades of the cross-cutter that was used to crop cloth. It is on display at Dunkirk Mill, Nailsworth.

on wheels and added a handle, you could use it to cut grass; in 1830 he patented his new invention, the lawnmower, an example of which can be seen in Stroud's Museum in the Park.

By the early 1800s virtually all aspects of turning wool from the sheep into cloth had been mechanised. The other important change affected the way in which that machinery was powered.

Chapter Eight

Power for the Mills

In the early years of the industry, the only part of the process that was mechanised was the fulling mill. Later, as more machinery came into use, the water wheel still remained the main power source for some time. There had always been some discussion among millwrights as to which form of water wheel was the most efficient. Basically, there are four main types of wheel that rotate around a horizontal axis: the undershot, where the bottom of the wheel is turned by the mill stream; the overshot, where the water is brought to a point above the wheel and the water falls into 'buckets' set round the wheel, another version of which is the pitch-back, which turns in the opposite direction; and the breast shot, which as the name suggests is half way between the two. The issue was finally resolved in the eighteenth century by the civil engineer John Smeaton, who carried out a series of experiments that showed that the overshot was the most efficient and the undershot the least. To some extent, the choice of which type of wheel to use depended on the lie of the land and the position of the mill. It was not always possible to install an overshot wheel without collecting the water from a long way upstream and bringing it to the mill via a long leat. One of the essentials for any system used to work machinery is keeping a steady rate of flow. By creating mill ponds, the water could be released in a regular fashion by controlling sluice gates.

In the eighteenth century, a new source of power came into use; the steam engine. The early years of development were dominated by the engine first developed by Thomas Newcomen for pumping water out of mines. Basically,

The pitch-back waterwheel used to power fulling stocks at Higher Mill, Helmshore, now part of the Helmshore Mills Textile Museum.

it consisted of an overhead beam pivoted at the centre, from one end of which pump rods were suspended. The weight of the rods pulled that end of the beam down. What Newcomen designed was a system for pulling the rods back up. The opposite end of the beam was attached by a chain to a piston in an open-topped cylinder. Steam was forced into the cylinder below the piston, which was then sprayed with cold water. The steam condensed, creating a partial vacuum and air pressure pushed the piston down, lifting the rods. Pressure equalised, gravity took over again, the rods dropped back. The whole process then began again, and the beam nodded up and down and the rods rose and fell. It was fine for pumping, but of little interest to manufacturers. It was also very inefficient in terms of fuel use. One exception was at Shudehill, near Manchester. In 1783, a 30ft diameter water wheel was installed in a textile mill there, and two storage

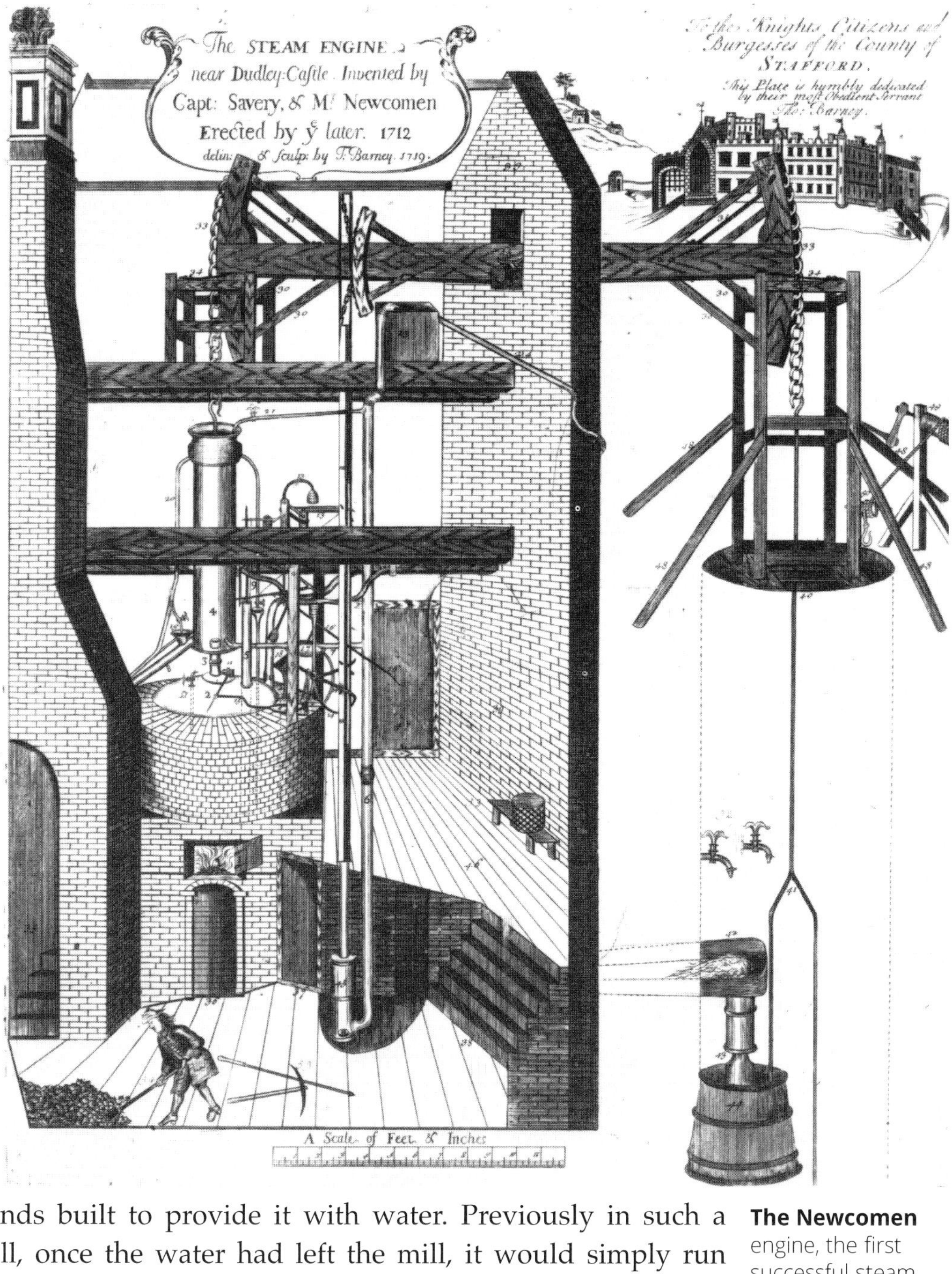

The Newcomen engine, the first successful steam engine, installed at a colliery in Didley in 1712.

ponds built to provide it with water. Previously in such a mill, once the water had left the mill, it would simply run away down to the river, but here a Newcomen type engine was installed to pump it back up to the reservoirs. It could be said to be the first steam engine to be used to work a mill, though it never worked any machinery directly. A few other mills used a similar system.

It was James Watt, at the time an instrument maker at Glasgow University, who spotted that the inefficiency was largely due to the energy wasted in reheating the cylinder at each stroke of the piston. His answer was to condense the steam in a separate vessel, so that the cylinder could be kept permanently hot. However, heat would still be lost through the open top, and if he closed that, then air pressure wouldn't push the piston down. His answer was to close the cylinder and use steam pressure both below and above the piston. The atmospheric engine was now a true steam engine. Its usefulness to mill owners, however, was still not obvious. The engine still required gravity to move the pump rods down. Although steam could raise the piston, it was still connected by a flexible chain – and you cannot use a chain to push anything up. A simple rod connecting beam and piston wouldn't work, because the end of the beam moved through the arc of a circle. Solving the problem of designing an engine that could both pull and push a piston was to Watt his greatest achievement – his parallel motion. The piston rod was not connected directly to the beam, but to one corner of a shifting parallelogram of rods – his parallel motion.

This was the great breakthrough. Watt now devised another system, where the steam engine could turn a wheel to supply power – just as the waterwheel did. This was his sun and planet gear. Instead of pump rods, the end of the beam was attached to a sweep arm that ended in a cog that ran around another cog attached to the wheel shaft. Watt had by now entered into a partnership with Matthew Boulton and one of their engines was installed at Robinson's cotton mill at Papplewick in Nottinghamshire in 1785. Other mills soon followed their lead, including woollen mills, and the cumbersome sun and planet mechanism was soon replaced by a simple crank at the end of the arm. The implications were enormous.

Crank Mill, Morley – the first woollen mill to install a steam engine in Yorkshire. The steam cylinder and the other half of the overhead beam are inside the engine house.

Anyone contemplating starting a new mill no longer had to look for a site with a guaranteed good water supply but could opt for sites near the best transport routes – and in the eighteenth century that meant next to one of the new canals. It would also make economic sense to be close to a productive coalfield. The Boulton & Watt engine was more efficient than the Newcomen but was still a ferocious consumer of fuel. In the past, periods of drought had effectively slowed or stopped production for a mill relying on water power. This was no longer a problem. The change was mainly felt in the north of England, where coal was plentiful. In the south west, the first steam engine was only installed at Wotton-under-Edge in 1802, and this and others that followed in the next few years were often only quite small powered engine intended to supplement water power, not replace it. The problem was that the cost of coal in the area was so much higher than in the north. Marilyn Palmer & Peter Neaverson in their book *The Textile Industry of South-West England,* 2005 quote figures for Trowbridge in 1815 as 24s 6d a ton, for Gloucestershire clothiers, who could get coal from the Forest of Dean via the Severn and the Stroudwater Canal, the coal was slightly cheaper at 21s, but Benjamin Gott at Armley Mill in Leeds was only paying as little as 14s a ton.

It is interesting following the fortune of one Gloucestershire mill – Dunkirk Mill – for the 100 years from the end of the eighteenth century. There is some uncertainly about when the first mill on the site was erected, possibly in the seventeenth century, but throughout most of the eighteenth century it was simply used as a fulling mill. Ian Mackintosh, one of the founders of the Stroudwater Textile Trust, has scoured the archives and unearthed a story that gives a strong indication of how clothiers felt about the advantages of mechanisation, steam and water power at the time.

The story starts in 1798, when John Cooper bought the mill and decided to start spinning using jennies to take advantage of the demand for cloth for uniforms in the Napoleonic Wars. He built a new block and installed two water wheels. By 1805, it was one of the biggest mills in the region, standing five storeys high, and a document recorded it as containing fulling stocks, a gig mill and 'machinery'. But Cooper went bankrupt and the mill was bought by members of the Playne family. William Playne brought in spinning machinery, added two new water wheels in 1816 and added a Boulton & Watt engine rated at just 14hp two years later. The mill developed as both a spinning and weaving mill, but it comes as a surprise to find that as late as 1839, there were just two power looms and sixty-seven hand looms. The Playne family argued that as long as the cloth could be produced as cheaply by hand as by machine, then it was better to give the jobs to the people not to the inanimate machines. By 1889, the mill then had four water wheels and two steam engines. But its days as the most important woollen mill in the area were coming to an end. Changes in fashion were the problem; the demand for woollen cloth had declined in favour of the lighter worsted. Over the next eighty years it was used variously for hosiery manufacture and making umbrellas and walking sticks.

What is clear from the story is that for a major manufacturer in the south west, steam was still of less importance than water power, even at the end of the nineteenth century. Most of the mill buildings have now been converted into flats, but part has been preserved as part of the area's rich heritage. One of the water wheels is still regularly turned and used to drive two machines in the Trust's museum area of the mill. It is an overshot wheel, 13ft in diameter and 12ft wide and seeing it lumber into motion always appeals to visitors. There is a small trickle of water, then gradually, the flow increases, the buckets begin to fill and then it starts rumbling into life. A calculation was made in 1900 of how much power this wheel would generate, and the answer came out as an impressive 74½hp. That makes the 14hp Boulton & Watt engine seem positively puny. One can see why it was tempting to continue to rely on water power, even though it left the mills of the south west at a disadvantage compared with those of Yorkshire.

Over the years, the performance of steam engines was greatly improved. High pressure steam came into use, which removed the need for a condenser. Compound engines were introduced in which the exhaust steam was not simply being allowed to escape into the atmosphere. It was still under pressure, so was passed to a second larger low-pressure cylinder. The overhead beam could be done away with. The cylinders could be horizontal instead of vertical, and the drive taken from the piston rod via a connecting rod to a crank. In these engines it was usual to have a large flywheel, with a grooved rim. Ropes fastened round the rim took the drive up to overhead shafts on every floor of the mill., From these shafts, belts were passed round pulleys and down to the machines. Engine houses were often quite highly decorated and the men who ran the engines were the new elite of the woollen industry. They were very much lords of their own domains, and no one came into their area without permission. As more and more engines were installed in mills, the textile

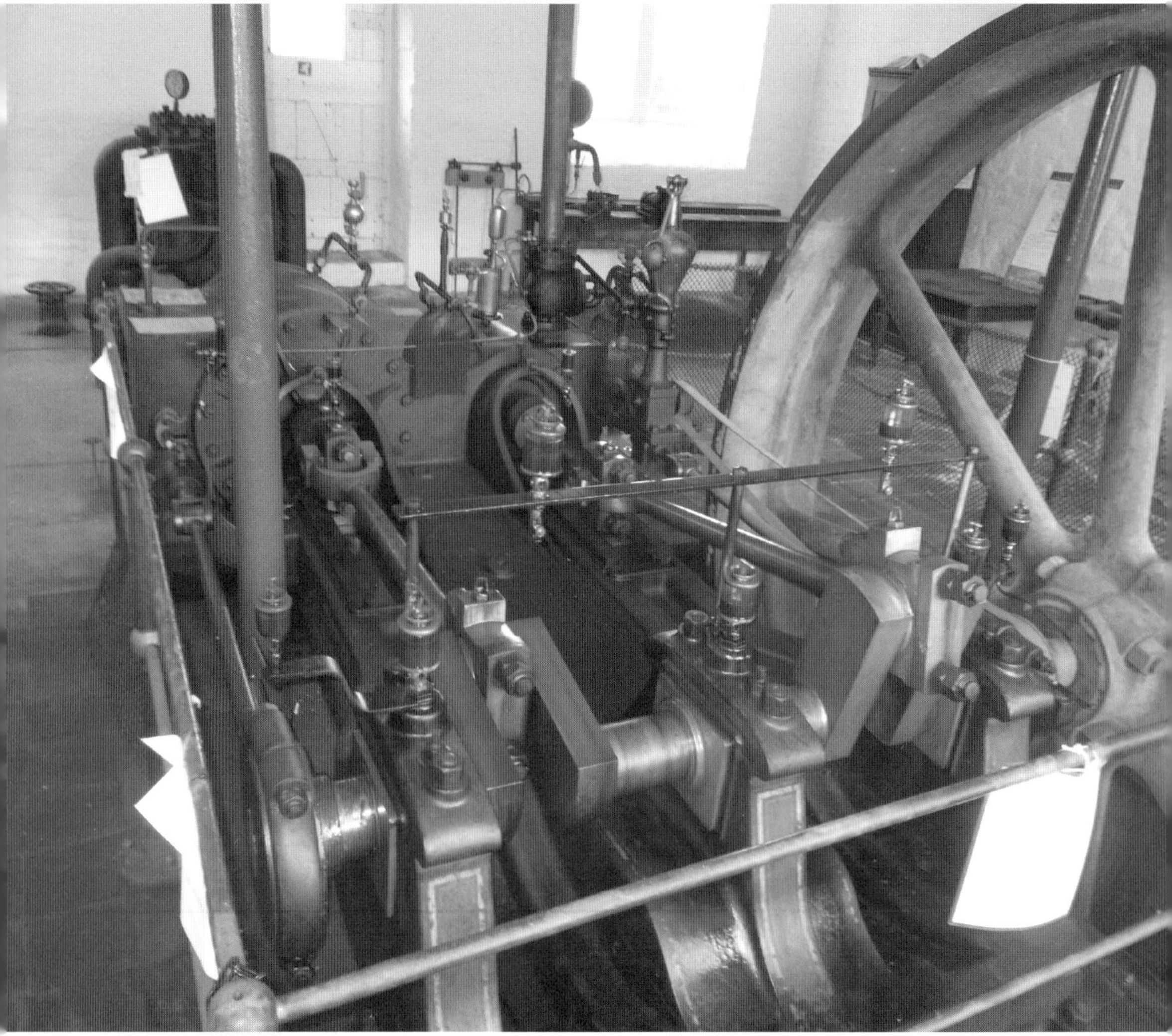

The Tangye steam engine at St. Mary's Mil, Chalford, Gloucestershire. Ropes round the grooves on the flywheel would have taken the drive to line shafting at every level of the mill.

towns of the North of England sprouted forests of chimneys, spreading a pall of smoke over the whole area.

Although in general the mills of the south west were less dependent on steam power than those of the rest of Britain, there was a notable exception. Coldharbour Mill at Uffculme in Devon is based on the site of a former water powered grist mill. The site was bought by Edward Fox in 1796 and a new woollen mill was built, originally water powered. It continued to rely solely on water power until 1865, when a beam engine was installed. As the company continued to prosper, this was replaced in 1910. An efficient Lancashire boiler was installed, and to ensure a good draught to the fire, a 125ft high chimney was built. The new engine was built by an important supplier of mill engines, Pollitt & Wigzell of Sowerby Bridge in Yorkshire. This is a two-cylinder compound engine. In order to balance the output from the two cylinders, the low pressure at 27in diameter has to be bigger than the 14½in high pressure cylinder. When installed it was rated at 240hp, but was later improved to 300hp. This is an immense increase compared with the modest engine installed at Dunkirk. The mill is now a working museum, and the engine has been preserved. Although the original beam engine has long gone, a replacement was supplied by the Science Museum. Both are steamed on special days of the year and provide a rare opportunity to see both types of mill engine at work. The mil is also unusual in having both carding and combing machinery.

Steam and water power drove mill machinery throughout the nineteenth century. A new source of power became available at the end of that time – electricity. It had a double advantage – individual machines could be turned on as required and electric lights could replace the old gas lights. There was a problem, however. With no national grid in existence, a mill that wanted electricity had to provide it from its own resources. Longford's Mill, Nailsworth, has long since become disused as a manufacturing unit, and many of the old buildings have been converted to residential use. The power house not only remains but has three generations of generators. The oldest is a steam engine, an unusual one in that the cylinders are enclosed in a metal case that is geared to turn the generator. Later this was replaced by a water turbine, fed by the extensive reservoir behind the mill and the final generator was worked by a diesel motor. All three are preserved but not, alas, open for public viewing. One mill, however, still does generate its own electricity. Trefriw woollen mill in North Wales has been run by the same family since 1859. It was originally powered by a conventional water wheel, but a water turbine was installed in the 1940s and is now exclusively used to provide the electricity for the spinning and weaving mill. As the present owner said, if they had to pay for their electricity, the business would simply not be viable.

This is a good place to pause to look at the different processes that took place in nineteenth-century mills between the arrival of the wool and the departure of finished cloth. Not every mill will include every stage of processing. When the wool arrived at the mill, it would have been compressed into tightly wadded bales. The fibres could be opened up by machine, usually a remarkably vicious-seeming device with large metal teeth that pulled the fibres apart. The wool might, when it arrived at the mill, need washing or scouring, and afterwards drying. In the south west of England, circular stone tower-like wool stoves were used in which the heat was supplied by a metal stove set in the centre. One of the few survivors is the stove built for Frogmarsh Mill, Woodchester, Gloucestershire, now extended and converted into a private house. These circular stoves seem to be limited to this area. In Yorkshire, for example, the drying houses were conventional long, low buildings in which the cloth was spread on a floor above boilers. At this stage, the wool might have been sent to the dye house, where it would be treated in vast cauldrons in scenes that might make a visitor think of the witches in *Macbeth*.

The wool would then be passed through a carding process that might involve two different stages. The first would be scribbling, which roughly disentangled the fibres. This process was mechanised in the late eighteenth century, leading in 1786 to a plea to manufacturers in the Leeds area

The wool drying stove at Frogmarsh Mill, Woodchester in 1973. It has now been converted into a family home.

of Yorkshire to stop using them – a plea which was, needless to say, ignored, but the printed address does give us a glimpse of the size of the industry at that time:

> The number of Scribbling-Machines extending about seventeen miles south south-west of LEEDS exceed all belief, being no less than one hundred and seventy! And as each machine will do as much work in twelve hours, as ten men can in that time do by hand (speaking within bounds) and they working night and day will do as much work as would otherwise employ twenty men.

From the scribbler, the material would pass to either the carding or combing machines.

After this it would be prepared as slubbings to feed to the spinner. The next stage might involve a slubbing billy, in the early years of the century, but this was later replaced by a number of different piecing machines or 'tommies'. The first was patented by J. Whittaker in 1827 and others followed, improving on the system. The carded wool was fed into one of a series of trays that was moved along when it contained the right amount of wool, and then fed the wool down to rubbing aprons that carried the strips away to be wound onto bobbins. An American inventor John Goulding produced a more sophisticated version at the even earlier date of 1822. His machine not only divided the carded wool into appropriate strips but twisted them into slubbings, ready for spinning.

The spun yarn would either be used for weft or warp, depending on its consistency. The weft wool would be loaded onto shuttles, but the warping process was more complex. It was simple enough for plain cloth but became more complex if patterns were needed. In either case, the bobbins were set on a frame and the yarn fed from them onto a rotating drum, round which they were wrapped. For a pattern, the different coloured warp threads had all to be arranged exactly in the right order, according to a previously worked out system. From the drum, the warp could now be transferred to the roller that fitted on the back of the loom. The warp threads would normally be dressed with some form of paste to provide extra strength.

Once the cloth had been woven, it would be sent for fulling. The fulling stocks were largely replaced in the nineteenth century by milling. Instead of being pounded by hammers, the cloth was sewn into a loop, which was passed through

A milling machine in which the wet cloth is pressed between rollers, performing the work previously done by fulling stocks.

rotating rollers inside a case. Originally the sewing would have been done by hand but large sewing machines were later introduced. This led to a bizarre accident in a Gloucestershire mill. The operative managed to get his finger between the needle and the cloth, and it went right through it. Nothing could be done until a mechanic could be found to dismantle the machine to take out the needle and in the meantime a lad was sent to bring a cup of tea to the unfortunate victim. He arrived, saw the scene and fainted. Another worker at the scene helped him up and gave him the tea. Eventually the sewer was released and went with the needle still stuck through his finger to the local hospital where it was removed. He was obviously a conscientious employee as he asked for the needle back as it was company property.

The cloth was taken away and inspected for any faults, which were corrected by hand. In the final stage it was pressed, packaged and sent away from the mill.

Chapter Nine

Cloth Varieties

So far, we have been looking at weaving cloth as though it was all much the same, but this was very far from being the case. In this chapter we shall be concentrating on the cloths woven in Britain. The demand for different types of cloth changed with the changes in fashion. In medieval Europe, both men and women wore full length garments. The wealthier male would wear what was known as a *cote-hardie* that buttoned down the front and women a full-length gown. Outdoor garments would be cloaks. Mostly these garments would be made from the heavy woollen broadcloth, and for outer garments it would indeed be heavy, weighing perhaps as much as 1½lb per yard. Wool was ubiquitous among the general population, but there was a time when they were not encouraged to compete with their betters. By the fourteenth century, fashions had begun to change, with British taste very much influenced by what was being worn in France – some things it seems, don't change all that much. Those who could afford to do so had exotic clothes dressed or lined with fur and cloth was regularly imported from Flanders. Edward III passed a number of sumptuary laws, including the Fur Act of 1337, which sought to ensure that the lower orders knew their place by decreeing that only the nobility, higher clergy and anyone with an annual income of over £100 could wear fur. The penalty was 'the forfeiture of the said R. And further to be punished at the King's Will.' He also decreed that only English wool could be worn. This was all an added boost to the broadcloth weavers of Britain.

Cloths of this period worn by yeomen and peasants had varieties that are unknown today. Kersey was a rough woollen cloth, which used a twill weave. This weave produces a distinctive pattern of diagonal ribs. The weft is passed over two or more warp threads, then under two or more. On the next line, the pattern is changed by moving it along a step to create the diagonals. The cloth appears to be named after Kersey in Suffolk but was more widely made. One of the best-known manufacturers was 'Jack of Newbury' – John Winchcombe. He employed between 30 and 50 weavers in his home town of Newbury in Berkshire and had a dye works, using vast quantities of woad – a single order was for 27 tons. He produced around 6,000 pieces of kersey a year. The size of a kersey was set by law. In 1465 it was defined as 'a yard and a nail' wide – a nail was 1/16 of a yard – and 18 yards long; this compares with broadcloths at 2 yards wide and 24 yards long. Much of Winchcombe's cloth was sent to London and then forwarded to the cloth fairs of Antwerp.

Burel was another rough cloth, known from medieval times, originally produced in ancient Gaul under the name 'bura'. Like kersey it is a twill weave, but this time the warp is either hemp or cotton and wool only appears in the weft. Worsted cloth is not dissimilar, apart from in the way in which the wool is treated before spinning. Worsted wool is combed, not carded. In this process, the comb is pulled through the fibres, during which the shorter fibres are removed.

By the seventeenth century, fashion had undergone further changes from the days of doublet and hose for men and elaborate farthingales for women that spread skirts so widely that it must sometimes have been difficult getting through a doorway. There was a general move towards lighter cloths. The British broadcloth manufacturers had a particular problem in that James I gave a monopoly for dyeing and finishing the cloth for export to William Cockayne. He was a London merchant, an alderman and at the same time chairman of the Eastland Company, that had received a royal charter for trading with the Baltic countries and Scandinavia.

Previously most cloth had been sent to Holland where it was dyed and finished, but under the new scheme, it was expected that the wool merchants would gain higher profits, and the crown would benefit by increasing taxes on the higher value cloth. The scheme backfired badly when the Dutch banned the import of British cloth. It was something of a fiasco, but dd not prevent the king from awarding Cockayne a knighthood two years later.

The development of serge as a material received a boost thanks to the religious wars of Europe, when many protestants came for refuge in Britain, including experienced serge weavers. This is another twill weave, this time with a two over, two under pattern. One place where they settled was Bradford-on-Avon which became a prosperous wool town, when the Bradford in Yorkshire was little more than a village. They were brought to the town by Paul Methuen and the wealth the trade created can be seen in the three terraces of houses constructed by the Methuen family on the hillside to the north of the town – Newtown, Middle Rank and Top Tory. Methuen profited greatly from this new enterprise ad became known as 'the greatest cloathier of his time'. The lighter serges were made using combed worsted for both warp and weft. When by the eighteenth century men started wearing breeches and jackets, the demand for the lighter materials grew even greater.

The name 'twill' has already cropped up a few times and must have been familiar to anyone in the business. In Scotland, the spelling was different – it was 'tweel'. So, it appears that in the 1830s, when consignment of tweel from Hawick reached the London merchant James Locke, he managed to misread it and marketed the cloth as 'Tweed'. The name stuck, Scottish tweed proved especially popular with country sportsmen and gamekeepers, as the soft colours produced by using natural dyes blended well with the colours of the countryside, providing anyone out shooting with a form of camouflage. The best known of all Scottish tweed is Harris. Cloth had been woven in the Hebrides long before the name 'Tweed' appeared as a description, mainly for local consumption. But in the 1840s the potato blight that caused mass starvation in Ireland had an equally devastating effect in the Hebrides. Much of the island of Harris was owned by the Dunmore family and Lady Dunmore decided to try to help. She ordered a tweed in the family tartan and showed it off to wealthy friends, who followed her example. This provided immediate relief, but also created a continued demand for tweed from the island. Other manufacturers began producing tweed cloth that was given the Harris name, even if they were working miles away from the island. In 1906, the Harris Tweed Association Ltd. was formed and soon established a legal trademark. Now a cloth could only be sold as Harris tweed if it satisfied specific requirements. Today the rules specify that the wool has to be Scottish and all the processes from carding to finishing have to be carried out in the Hebrides. Woollen mills were set up in the region for spinning and finishing, but weaving remains a cottage industry. Not only does the loom have to be in the weaver's home, but power has to be supplied by means of a foot treadle. It is not exactly, handloom weaving in the old way, but close to it, and seeing an 87-year-old still weaving in the converted garage next to his house, it seems the exercise does no one any harm.

While on the subject of twill woven fabrics in Scotland, it is worth pausing to look at that most famous of Scottish garments, the kilt, traditionally woven from wool in this way. Its origins are much disputed, but it would appear that it had become a common form of dress in the Highlands by the sixteenth century. But this was not the kilt we know today – it was the Feildean Mor in Gaelic, the great kilt, a woollen garment normally draped over one shoulder and reaching down to the knees, the upper part of which could be unfolded to make a cloak in bad weather. The earliest descriptions do not mention tartans as being an essential part of the garment. The origin of the short kilt is said to be tied up with a new industrial complex. Thomas Rawlinson was an English Quaker, who set up an ironworks at Invergarry near Inverness in 1729. Given the nature of the work, he thought the bulky great kilt was too dangerous to wear, so he designed a shortened version with sewn-in pleats, the walking kilt. Needless to say, many Scots vehemently deny that their national dress was invented by an Englishman, and I certainly wouldn't want argue the point at a Burns Dinner! Following the quelling of the Jacobite rebellion at Culloden in 1746, the wearing of the kilt was forbidden by law. The Highlanders tended to be looked down on by Lowland Scots – you can get a very good idea of how they regarded them by reading James Boswell's account of his travels round Scotland with Dr Johnson. As kilt making stopped, so too did the weaving of clan tartans, and old patterns were lost, weavers who understood them died and the tradition might never have been revived but for a visit to Edinburgh by George IV, who suggested that those invited to attend official functions should wear the appropriate tartans. Edinburgh tailors and weavers had a roaring trade providing 'authentic' clan tartans. Today, tartans are officially authenticated by the Registers at Lyon Court. One of the few weavers using traditional methods to make tartan cloth for kilts is D.C. Dalgleish of Selkirk. The 'small' loom requires 1630 warp threads, that need to be just over ten yards long. As all kilt material is woven on the loom, the new thread can simply be tied onto the threads left behind from the last finished length. The loom itself is similar to that used in Harris, but the foot pedal has been motorised.

Another famous tweed is Donegal. The story really begins in 1866 when John Magee began employing weavers. At first, they were working at home, but later he set up a factory with handlooms and later converted to power looms. The company remains the leading supplier of the typical 'salt and pepper' speckled tweed. But the old tradition has also been revived. In the 1990s, Denis Mulhern, a fifth-generation handloom weaver, set up Triona Design in Ardara, Donegal to manufacture tweed on handlooms.

Blankets are not an especially different form of cloth, but they have an interesting history. The idea of using thick woollen material as a bed covering instead of animal hides was reputedly first introduced into Britain by a Flemish weaver called Blanquette, who went to work in Bristol, and whose name became anglicised into 'blanket'. Among the first and most important centres of production was Witney in Oxfordshire. Records show the Earl of Leicester as buying thirty blankets there in 1584. A century later in 1681 a Witney manufacturer reached an agreement with the Hudson Bay Company to supply them with blankets. This proved to be highly profitable, but soon developed into a wider trade. In the eighteenth century, the Canadian company began buying in 'point blankets', so called because of the black lines woven into the selvage. They had brightly coloured stripes and were traded with the native Canadian and American population in exchange for beaver pelts. The Navajos, however, decided to set up in business weaving for themselves, and an American blanket company was set up in Oregon, on the famous Oregon trail, also producing blankets for trading. The blanket cloth itself was developed from broadcloth production, but where in the latter the nap was raised and then cut, with blankets the nap was left uncut to give a fluffy finish. The first teasel raising gig, or 'blanket rower' as it was known there was introduced into Witney in 1782 and was powered by a horse, Witney remained famous for blankets until its last mill closed in 2002. The other major centre for English blankets was Yorkshire where, happily, production still continues. The John Atkinson works at Pudsey have been in the business since the 1780s.

The trade was originally regulated through the Company of Blanket Makers. In 1721 the Company built Blanket Hall, where they held their meetings, and to which all Witney blankets were brought to be weighed and approved, a custom that continued until 1815. The Hall itself still remains and is open to the public. The Master of the Company in 1711 was Thomas Early, and Early's continued manufacturing blankets until 2002, when the equipment was bought by Quiltex of Derbyshire. One of the oldest survivors from the Witney industry is a blanket loom that was in use in the first decade of the eighteenth century, but was 'modernised' c.1800 by the addition of a flying shuttle. It has found a home far from Witney at Fairfield Mill at Sedbergh in Cumbria.

Blanket looms at a mill in Worcester, Massachusetts in 1918. They were being used to make blankets for the army and the Red Cross.

Another bed covering that used wool was the Welsh quilt. The decorative cover was stuffed with wool, but the cover itself would have been made using whatever scraps of material were available. In the eighteenth and nineteenth centuries, this would often be flannel. The patterns would usually be quite bold, but it was up to the individual quilters to make their own variations. For a time, it became a profitable cottage industry. The quilts themselves can now be seen more as works of art than as useful things to keep one warm in bed.

Flannel is a cloth usually made from short fibre carded wool and is often brushed on one or sometimes both sides to nap it. The name is thought to have originated in Wales, where the cloth was made in the sixteenth century, but the name 'flanelle' was definitely in use in France in the seventeenth century. Wales became a major centre for its manufacture and specialist carding mills were established in the eighteenth century. One is still remembered in the name Carding Mill Valley, an area on the Welsh border between Shropshire and Powys. The industry developed in Newport and Llanidloes in the nineteenth century with large steam-powered spinning and weaving mills. Flannel had a ready market for making shirts and underwear for the workers in the heat of the country's iron, steel and tinplate industries.

Among the many varieties of cloth are some that are highly specialised and few more so than billiard cloth. I live in Stroud, an area once packed with working mills that now has just this one working survivor. Lodgemore Mill near the town centre is just one of the few manufacturers of this specialised material and they have been making billiard cloth since the 1860s. What is it that makes this cloth special? The most obvious factor is its width. The local company manufacture cloth that will be able to cover the largest competition snooker tables, which are 12ft by 6ft. As you cannot have a stitched seam in the middle of the table, the cloth has to be woven on very wide looms. The cloth must not only be large but completely uniform. The inspiration is said to have come from coachmen's capes that had a nap running from the shoulder to the hem, helping to shed the rainwater. Billiard cloth too has a one-way nap. Only the finest wool is used, originally imported from Germany, but is now Merino wool, mostly from Australia. The nap raising and later shearing have to be done with the greatest precision to get the perfect surface. That cloth for billiard and snooker tables is traditionally green, as opposed to the usual blue for pool, said to derive from the colour of those coachmen's cloaks. One thing, however, it absolutely is not; it is not baize. That is a mixture of wool and cotton, not pure wool.

Not all cloth manufacturing started with natural wool taken directly from the fleece. There was a thriving recovered wool

Weaving billiard cloth on very wide looms at Ham Mill, Gloucestershire.

industry in Yorkshire, mainly concentrated around the towns of Batley, Dewsbury and Morley. Waste material such as rags and tailors' clippings were brought to the mills to be sorted by colour and type. Once they were sorted, any non-woollen material had to be removed, such as cotton stitching. The material was then torn apart in machines called 'devils', very similar to those used for opening up the wool from compressed bales. The end result was a mass of fibres that could be sent for spinning. In 1859, C. Garnett introduced a new machine in which saw-like teeth were set in spiral grooves round rotating cylinders. This enabled closely-knit 'hard' fabrics as well as soft fabrics to be processed. The fibres from the former went to make shoddy, the latter to make mungo.

All the cloths described here have been made from sheep's wool, but cloth in Britain was also produced using the fleeces of other animals, such as alpacas. That's something we shall be looking at later.

Chapter Ten

A Changing World

It is usual to speak of the early stages of cloth manufacture in Britain as being a cottage industry, but that does not mean that the organisation was entirely haphazard nor that the cottages themselves were all organised in the same way. One tends to think of the typical weaver's cottage as being one with the loom workshop as the top floor of a three storey building. This was largely true of the north of England, but even so there were variations. Some terraces of cottages had continuous workshops that ran right across the top of the row. These was often no direct access from the living quarters, with the loom shop either entered via an external staircase, or from the upper level when the row was built against the hillside. In some cases, the workers' cottages can be seen grouped round a clothier's house and would have been rented out by him. There is a good example at Almondbury, once an important town in its own right, but now engulfed by Huddersfield. The main house is quite opulent and well built, while the surrounding cottages must have been quite cramped, as they are only two storeys high, but the 'weavers' windows' on the upper floor show that the living space was limited to the ground floor. Things appear even more cramped in the village of Kirkpatrick Durham which, in spite of its name, is actually in Kirkcudbrightshire in Scotland. Here an estate was built on his own ground by the Rev. David Lamont in 1785. The single storey cottages are spread out down the main road. At the opposite extreme is the village of Dilton Marsh in Wiltshire. Dilton was an old settlement, but at the end of the seventeenth century there was a haphazard spread of cottage building on the wasteland of the Marsh – some cottages had workshops built in, others housed looms in outbuildings, tacked onto the sides of the houses.

It has to be remembered when looking at these survivors from the age of handloom weaving, that not all weavers had distinctive homes. There are many towns and villages where weavers were known to work in large numbers, but where physical signs are entirely absent as far as the workers themselves are concerned. Some are even deceptive. The famously picturesque row of cottages, Arlington Row in Bibury Gloucestershire are well known as weavers' cottages, and they might have been thought to have been built as

Former weavers' cottages at Golcar near Huddersfield, with the typical long mullioned windows on the top floor which was the loom workshop. Spinning and carding would have taken place on the ground floor.

such. In fact, this was originally a single building, a monastic wool store built in 1380 and converted into cottages in the seventeenth century. In the early years of the hosiery industry, stocking frames were used in homes that are only notable for the very large windows on the ground floor – glass was too expensive to be used for big windows unless the extra light was necessary for the work going on inside. There are examples in Calverton, where the Rev. Lee invented the frame.

Opponents of the factory system tended to provide a somewhat idealised version of life in the cottages of the handloom era. Gregory King made an estimate of the numbers and people of England and Wales in 1688 and he divided them into two main categories, those who were increasing the wealth of the nation, and those decreasing it. Those who were decreasing it were not the idle wealthy, holders of sinecures and the like, but the hard-working poor, unable to make enough to live on from their labours. According to King, out of an estimated population of five and a half million, nearly thee million were decreasing the wealth. Many weavers had supplemented their income by keeping perhaps a few geese or even a cow on the common land, but Enclosure Acts had fenced in the common, drained the land and turned it to arable farming and private ownership. Defoe reported in his travels that 'The common people all over this country, not only are poor, but look poor; they appear dejected and discouraged, as of they had given up all hopes of ever being otherwise than what they are'. It is hardly a picture of a rural idyll.

When work began to shift from cottage to mill, one of the arguments in favour of employing children was that they had always worked with their families in the home. There is, however, a fundamental difference between working within a family unit and trudging off each day for the relentless work of the mill. The cotton mills that were the first to introduce spinning and later weaving often relied heavily on apprentices. Many of these were sent by parishes who wanted to be rid of children on poor relief, which had to be paid by the parish. They were happy to make a one-off payment to the mill owner rather than paying to continue keeping the children fed and clothed. Conditions in the apprentice houses varied considerably, but the system never applied to any very great degree to the woollen industry. One reason was that it soon became clear that it was not economically very successful. Many mill owners found that it was cheaper to pay a small wage than to go to all the trouble of looking after and feeding the children themselves. Most children in the woollen mills were employed directly and paid wages. The most complete record of child labour in woollen mills comes from the !833 Government Report on children in mills and mines.

The mill owners were sent a questionnaire requesting among other things, the number of boys and girls of different ages, how many hours were worked, when did they have meal breaks, punishments given out, how much were they paid, and holidays allowed. The Report is a huge document, but there is a certain uniformity in the answers. As an example, here are some of the answers from the Huddersfield area and the Colne Valley. Few mills employed anyone under the age of ten and the ratio of child labour to adult labour varied enormously from mill to mill. In some of the smaller mills, the ratio might be half below the age of eighteen and half above, but in major concerns such as Stables out of 275 workers, only 49 were under eighteen. One employer wrote that 'No part of my works requires children under twelve years of age; the reason for children under twelve being employed, is the application of their parents, and coming with the older children, till they will not stay at home to be idle, and take half work like the rest.' Another stated, 'It would be a great hardship upon those who have a numerous family if they were not allowed to earn anything until they were twelve,' a statement that does not say much about the wages paid if families have to rely on the youngest going to work to survive.

The hours worked were long, some of the most arduous conditions being reported at one mill where work started at 6am and only ended at 8.15 pm. In most mills, work stopped at 5 in the afternoon on Saturdays, and no work was done on Sundays. The workers had half an hour for breakfast at 8, an hour for lunch and a half hour break in the afternoon. This pattern was repeated over and over again. In some mills, the machinery was stopped for the meal breaks, but not in all. One owner reported that most of his work involved power looms and, as they were not stopped, the weavers had to eat as and when they could. In another, children employed in scribbling had to attend the machines all the time and could only have meal breaks by changing places for brief periods. In general, there were few holidays, apart from a few days at Christmas and Easter and there was no holiday pay. Similarly, anyone falling sick received no pay until they came back to work, though one owner did proudly point out that he kept the job open for them. One surprising finding was the entry for John Wrigley & Sons, who had a mill powered by a 33hp steam engine and specialised in scribbling, carding, milling and fulling. All the work of spinning and weaving was done outside. Of the estimated 1,000 inhabitants of the local village, 400 were employed by Wrigley in spinning and weaving. Wrigley did, however, add a comment to his report:

> For more than fifty years that I have lived in the village, I always thought the working classes quite as comfortable as in any place I knew until the Beer Bill passed into law and four beer-shops opened in and near the village, which have done mischief enough, in making men who before that were sober into drunkards.

The Act of 1830 allowed anyone to brew and sell beer after paying two guineas for a licence. Its main object was to woo people off the ruinous habit of drinking gin.

Most owners said they did not punish the children physically, but simply sacked any who misbehaved. At Holmfirth mill, though, the owners wrote, 'Corporal punishments are inflicted on all the children employed in the mill; and it is necessary to punish them in that way, as long as they are worked so many hours per day, otherwise their work would be ill-performed'. In that mill, the hours were from 5am to 9pm and one can only assume that beatings were necessary simply to keep the children from dropping asleep at their workplace. When asked to comment on whether legislation was necessary, most owners agreed with this typical comment: 'We are of the opinion that in the woollen business there is no occasion for the legislature to regulate the hours.' The Gartsides of Holmfirth mill, however, expressed a very different view. 'The system of working, as at present conducted, is one of cruelty and degradation; it is even disgusting to any man of humanity, whether he be a mill proprietor or not; but the humane are bound to practice it so long as it is the general practice.' No one, it seems, could afford to stop employing children and putting higher paid adults in their place if they wished to remain competing with those who kept to the old system with its lower labour costs. The results for Gloucestershire were not dissimilar to those from Yorkshire, though the Dunkirk Mill report contained the curious statement that though the mill supervisors never hit the children, the parents were allowed to do so if the children misbehaved.

One area that was not covered by the Report was safety for the children working among what was mostly unguarded machinery. Yet horrific injuries did occur, some fatal, as this coroner's report of an accident at Ebley Mill, Gloucestershire in 1809 testifies:

> On view the body of David Pearce, aged about 8 years, who was killed by getting entangled in a scribbling engine, at

This well-known illustration is actually of a cotton mill, but the mules in a woollen mill would have been much the same, and children would still be required to crawl around among the moving machinery. It is taken from Edward Baines' history of the cotton industry of 1835.

> the manufactory of S. Clissold Esq. at Ebley; he was wound round the shaft of the machine with such velocity that his head, legs and right arm were literally torn from his body.

Eventually parliament did act on age and hours of working, though the attempts to pass a bill produced heated opposition. One memorable speech on the subject was made by William Cobbett in favour of Lord Ashley's Bill, for limiting the hours for mill children, as reported in Hansard:

> Heretofore, we have sometimes been told that our ships, our mercantile traffic with foreign nations by means of those ships, together with our body of rich merchants; we have sometimes been told that these form the source of our

> wealth, power and security. At other times, the land has stepped forward, and bid us look to it, and its yeomanry, as the sure and solid foundation of our greatness and our safety. At other times, the Bank has pushed forward her claims, and has told us, that great as the others were, they were nothing without 'PUBLIC CREDIT', upon which, not only the prosperity and happiness, but the very independence of the country depended. But, Sir, we have this night discovered that the shipping, the land, and the Bank and its credit, are all nothing worth compared with the labour of three hundred thousand little girls in Lancashire! Aye, when compared with only an eighth part of the labour of these three hundred thousand little girls, from whose labour, if we only deduct two hours a day, away goes the wealth, away goes the capital, away go the resources, the power and the glory of England!

The hope had been to reduce the work of children in all mills – not just the cotton mills of Lancashire – to a maximum of ten hours a day. In the event, it was something of a mixed bag. It specified that no children could be employed under the age of nine. Nine to 12 year-olds were only to work for 8 hours a day, and 13 to 18 years old restricted to 12 hours. The under-thirteens were to receive 2 hours schooling a day, part payment for which was to come from their wages. To enforce this, inspectors were appointed, but as there were only four at first, required to monitor some 4,000 mills, evasion of the law was simple. Although there were several other Acts making adjustments to working conditions, the minimum age for employing children was not raised to 10 until 1874.

What was notable about the 1833 survey was the reliance of virtually every mill in the Yorkshire area on steam power. This meant that mills were scattered over a large area and in the major towns, they would be built all round the central area. Some years ago, I was offered a trip by helicopter down the Colne valley, following the line of the river and the Huddersfield Narrow Canal from Marsden to Huddersfield itself. A pattern developed, with mills taking advantage of canalside sites at first. There was a small cluster of mills in Marsden, then an isolated mill built right alongside the canal on the approach to Slaithwaite, with a contemporary terrace of houses, but the real change came when we reached Huddersfield itself, where the mills simply appeared as a jumble, with the River Colne and the canal running through the middle, with tall spinning mills and adjacent low weaving sheds and a forest of tall chimneys. Squeezed in between was a scattering of terraced houses. This was a new type of townscape, that was repeated throughout the West Riding of Yorkshire. Tall chimneys came to dominate the landscape, but none ever approached the one originally built in the 1870s for J.E. Wainwright's dye works in Halifax. It is 275 ft high and very ornate and Wainwright eventually decided to convert it into an observatory with viewing platforms. If he ever went to the top platform, he must have been a fit man – there are 405 steps to get there. Its role as a chimney has long been over, and it is now simply known as Wainwright's Tower and is a tourist attraction.

Bradford, for example, was transformed. In 1810, there was a population of around 16,000 and five steam-powered mills were recorded. By 1840, there were 120 worsted mills and the population had grown to nearly 70,000. It was not yet a city, but it was a town with pretentious to grandeur. The town hall, built in 1873, was a conscious attempt to match the Gothic splendour of the great halls of northern Europe. Six years earlier, the town got its wool exchange, which might not be as exotic outside, but the interior is quite extraordinary. This is a pantheon dedicated to secular gods. They are ranged around the main hall: Raleigh and Columbus, who opened up world trade; the inventors, Arkwright, Watt and Jacquard; politicians, Palmerston and Gladstone. One outstanding figure is Cobden, who stands beside the motto 'free trade, peace, goodwill among nations'. The marble pillars are all numbered, very useful in the days when the hall would have been crowded with traders, and it would have been very convenient to be able to say 'I'll see you by column twelve at noon'. Bradford thrived on international trade, and a whole area of the town was given over to grand warehouses and merchants' offices, and a surviving complex is still known as Little Germany. One of these belonged to the Delius family from Germany who had a son, Fritz who was more interested in music than commerce. He later changed his name and became famous as the composer Frederick Delius.

An aerial view of Huddersfield from the middle of the twentieth century, with mills surrounded by rows of terraced houses.

Walking around Bradford today is completely rewarding, but we are not seeing the Bradford of the nineteenth century, when a pall of smoke hung over everything. The city lies in a hollow, and there were times when coming down towards it all you would have seen was the tops of multiple chimneys, dribbling down their dark, sooty clouds. One man decided that the atmosphere of the town was so toxic that he would build a mill away from the grime and provide first class accommodation for the workforce. His name was Titus Salt, who in 1822 had gone into business as a partner with his father at the age of just nineteen. Their original aim had been to buy wool from Russia and sell it to Bradford spinners for worsted. No one was interested, so they set up their own spinning business. In 1833, the father retired, leaving Titus in sole control. Three years later, he was visiting Liverpool where several bales of alpaca were being sold off cheaply, because no one seemed interested in buying the material, He took samples away to try spinning them and when that was successful, he bought the shipment. Over the next few years, he made a highly successful career in working with mohair and alpaca, becoming the largest employer in Bradford, with six mills in the town. In 1850, when he was made mayor of Bradford, he began his plans for his new mill and mill town, near Shipley on the River Aire, that would be called Saltaire.

He employed the Bradford architects Lockwood and Mason to design the whole complex, and the famous mill engineer William Fairbairn to lay out the mill. It was to be an integrated mill and a masterpiece of organisation. Built close to the river Aire and the Leeds and Liverpool Canal, a five-storeyed warehouse with loading doors opening directly onto the canal. Here the wool was sorted then taken to the next building for washing, drying and combing. The mill building for spinning was also five storeys high with a basement and the spun yarn was then moved on to the weaving sheds. Power was supplied by two beam engines. Everything was organised so that process followed process in a smooth, orderly fashion. A dye house was added later. The style was Italianate with chimneys in the style of campaniles.

The same architects were also given the job of designing the accompanying village. All the houses were intended to be rented and their style and size reflected the status of the occupants. There were taller boarding houses at the ends of terraces and bigger houses for overseers and even grander buildings for the company's executives. Originally there were to be 700 cottages laid out on a regular grid, and everything followed the same Italianate style as the mill. It was a wonderfully healthy place compared with Bradford just a few miles away, with wide roads, gardens, recreation grounds and a whole range of public buildings. There was a works dining hall, bath houses and wash houses, schools, almshouses, a mechanics institute, a music room and a church. One building was notably absent – there was no pub. Titus Salt was no teetotaller, keeping an excellent cellar for himself and his guests. He was, however, almost paranoid on worker control. Pubs were places where anyone could meet and discuss matters such as pay – Saltaire generally paid less than Bradford mills, but more than compensated by the improved amenities. There were strict restrictions on large gatherings. Salt was undoubtedly benevolent, but he was also more than a little despotic.

In time, Saltaire expanded and there was something of a problem in getting people into houses appropriate to their rank if they got promoted. This problem was solved with an ingenious idea. It was not just the size of house that showed a worker's status but the numbers of panels on the front door. The family might not get a better house with promotion, but they would have a new front door. Production at the mill stopped in 1983 and the mill buildings now contain a variety of shops and a gallery showing art donated by local born artist David Hockney. The village itself has been preserved and Saltaire is now a world heritage site.

In Scotland, tweed dominated the woollen trade, as it still does. Crombie began making cloth at a mill on the River Don at Cothall, working not just with wool but also vicuna from the Andes and cashmere. In 1859 they built a new, much larger mill at Grandholme also on the Don, near Aberdeen. It was the largest mill in Scotland and at the start of the twentieth century was employing 1,400 workers. It was noted for the fine quality of the product, and soon they were sending out labels to the tailors making garments identifying them as genuine Crombies. The Crombie overcoat was worn by British royalty and prime ministers, even John F. Kennedy favoured the coat. In the 1960s it was popular music royalty that set a fashion, when the Beatles appeared in Crombies, which became the must-have garment for the Mods of the sixties. This was an exception. Scottish woollen mills tended to be largely small concerns, mostly situated in the Borders. As late as the 1850s, over eighty per cent of the mills relied on water power. Even in the most important mill towns, such as Galashiels, there was still a heavy reliance on water power. In 1863, sixteen of the eighteen mills were still using it as the main power source, with steam of only secondary importance. One result of this scattering of mills was that the area never suffered from the overcrowding and pollution of major English mill towns. The same could be said of the mills of South West England and Wales.

The larger mills that came to dominate the main woollen areas were made possible by an important change in construction when the iron frame came to replace the wooden frame of the earlier mills. None of the earlier Yorkshire mills was more than 30ft wide, the maximum distance that timber beams could span without extra supports. The introduction of cast iron columns appeared towards the end of the eighteenth century. This was an ideal material, being strong in compression and was readily available from the new generation of coke fired furnaces.

Cast iron beams and trusses were not so successful, being heavy and difficult to install. The puddling process for converting cast iron pigs into wrought iron made the latter widely available and now iron frames could be constructed using a mixture of the two, with cast iron for structures in compression and wrought iron for beams and trusses. The mills of the nineteenth century began to look very different from their predecessors, not only bigger but often more elaborately ornamented. This can be seen, for example, in a magnificent iron framed buildings in Gloucestershire, Stanley Mill. Seen from the outside it may not seem very special, although unusual for this part of the world in being built of brick rather than stone. The interior, however, astonishes. Built in 1813, the construction followed an earlier pattern, with hollow cast iron columns and iron and brick arches supporting the floors. It could all have been quite plain, but instead the connecting arches have distinctive tracery patterns, and as the load decreased on the upper floors, so slender pillars replaced the bulkier pillars lower down. The decorative ironwork was extended to other details, such as the Venetian windows and fanlights above doors. The mill remained in use until quite recently, but at the time of writing stands empty, waiting for a new use.

In America, the woollen industry never began to match the importance of cotton manufacture, and was almost entirely centred in New England. The biggest change came at the end of the nineteenth century. Frederick Ayer had mills in both Lawrence and Lowell, Massachusetts. Together with his son-in-law William Wood, he formed the American Woolen Company, and gradually began buying up more and more mills until they owned around 60, employing some 4,000 workers, many of them recent immigrants. With competition greatly reduced and with the help of government-imposed tariffs on foreign imports, the company prospered, able to command high prices. Little of that prosperity reached the workforce of Lawrence, where the company had eight mills. A report of 1910 seems reminiscent of the reports written in Britain in the early years of the industrial revolution. Mortality rates were appalling, especially among the children once they reached the mills. A local doctor, Elizabeth Shapleigh, reported that many died within two to three years of starting work and that about a third of the whole workforce died by the age of 25. The homes were mostly wooden multi-storey apartment blocks, belonging to the company and packed close together. An official report of 1912 included this telling anecdote. 'The houses are so close in these half-blocks that it is said to have been the practice of one agent to collect the rents at the third and fourth stories by reaching out into the apartments on the same floor in the next houses.' The Labor Commission officially set the living wage at $8.28 a week; a third of Lawrence workers were earning less than $7. Families lived on bread, molasses and beans and a day with meat was 'like going on holiday'. In January 1912, the Industrial Workers of the World (IWW) Union called a strike. Organisation was in the hands of a committee of ten, only one of whom had actually been born in America.

The police were joined by locally recruited militias to oppose the strikers. On 29 January, a strikers' march was cornered – a shot rang out and one of the strikers, Annie le Pizzo, was killed. The police declared that the shot had really been aimed at them and arrested Joseph Caruso, charging him with murder. They also arrested two of the leaders of the strike for abetting him, even though they were literally miles away at the time, on the grounds that they had incited violence. As the strike continued, arrangements began to be made for the children to be moved to helpers in other towns and cities, where they could be looked after and well fed. When the first group arrived at Grand Central Station, New York they were met by a crowd of around 1,000 and marched away in a

Mills lining the Merrimack River at Lawrence, Massachusetts.

triumphant parade. A poem, published at the time in the *New York Call* gives an idea of the mood of the time.

Was it an army's martial tread
That beat through the traffic's sullen roar
And was it the shouting of warriors dread
That the icy blast of North wind bore?

Nay 'twas the patter of little feet
And children's voices clear and sweet
Loud sang their call o'er the city's din
'We are the strikers and we will win!'

The authorities in Lawrence tried to prevent any more children being sent away to avoid giving the strikers any more opportunities to stage such marches. When the authorities did arrive to stop the children leaving, there was a scuffle at the station resulting in many women being arrested. Most refused to pay the fines imposed by the court and were jailed, some taking their young children with them. It attracted a swathe of adverse criticism. Some students from Ivy League Universities had volunteered to join anti-strike militias – Harvard gave them official leave to do so. Now many other students, especially in women's colleges, began fund raising for the strikers. On 12 March the IWW entered into negotiations and the workers won nearly all their demands. After the strike was over, the three accused were put on trial – all were acquitted.

There is a postscript to the Lawrence story. In the 1920s, William Wood opened a new mill at Shawsheen, where he created a model village. There were two categories of house, either white wooden with green shutters for middle management or brick for senior executives. There was, however, no provision for the workers, who still had to remain in overcrowded Lawrence and come to work by streetcar. Today, the American Woolen Company has survived, after several takeovers, but is now limited to a single mill complex at Stafford Springs, Connecticut, where they spin and weave worsted wool, camel hair and cashmere.

Chapter Eleven

Carpets and Rugs

There is no intrinsic difference between carpets and rugs as far as making is concerned. In modern usage, a carpet covers a whole floor area, a rug just part of it. The earliest surviving rugs were found in Kazakhstan in 1949, encased in ice in the tomb of a Scythian nobleman. These are known as the Pazyryk rugs and recent research has revealed that they were created in the fifth century BCE. They are similar and the following details are for one of these, now in the Hermitage Museum, St. Petersburg, fragments of which were analysed for the dating process. This is a woollen knotted rug. The basis for the carpet is a plain weave to which the knots are added. In this case, the Ghiordes, symmetrical or Turkish knot was used. The knot yarn is passed over two warp threads, brought back under one, wrapped round them both and then pulled through, after which the ends are cut and these form the pile of the rug, and the knot is then pushed home. This was all done by hand and was a laborious process – there are 3,600 knots for every 10cm square of the rug. It was not simply a matter of tying knots, but the appropriate thread for each knot had to be selected to create the pattern. And as can be seen from the reproduction of the rug in the Hermitage, in which the pattern is clearer than in the ancient original (colour section) this is a very intricate affair. All round the outside is a border containing horsemen and their mounts and inside that, depictions of twenty-four elks, with geometric shapes filling the rest of the space. A curious feature of the elks is that their internal organs are also shown. Analysis of the 'Turkish red' dye used on the rug showed that it was produced by first fermenting the wool, then adding the dye itself made out of rose madder. This technique was widely used in Armenia, suggesting that might have been where it was made, though some experts have argued for a Persian origin.

Given the fineness of the workmanship and the complexity of the design, although this is the earliest complete rug or carpet ever discovered, there must have been simpler, plainer predecessors. The general view is that carpets were first made by nomadic people, a tradition that continued up to recent times, for example with those of the Middle East and North Africa who lived in tents made out of woven goat hair. In the tradition that was carried on into recent times, the weaving process was very basic. Two wooden battens were fixed on the ground to hold the warp thread in tension, after which the weft was added by hand. It is possible that this was a simple weave, but it is more likely that a knotting technique was used. It is only much later that we find actual carpets made in these regions, notably in Turkey and what was then Persia. There are hints of former glories in early Arabic chronicles and Byzantine envoys recorded seeing 22,000 splendid carpets at Abbasid Palace in Baghdad in 917. Carpet weaving was largely the work of women, but the grandest carpets, made for the court, were the work of master weavers and were based on the designs prepared for them by specialist artists. Among the finest ever produced were the two made in Ardabil in Persia, now Iran, one of which is preserved in the Victoria and Albert Museum in London (colour section).

The carpets were designed for the burial place of the Sufi leader, Shaykh Safi al-Din Ardabali, who died in 1334. This became a shrine for pilgrims and the carpets were made to enhance it, and we know the date of the one preserved in London, for woven into it is the inscription that declares it was 'the work of the slave of the portal' and the date 946 in the Muslim calendar, 1539-40 in ours. They would probably have remained in the mosque had the building not been severely damaged by an earthquake in 1873, when they were sold to raise funds for reconstruction. One was bought by a Manchester merchant. Among those who hugely admired it was William Morris and he persuaded the Victoria and Albert to buy it, which they did for £2,000 and it is now on display in a special case, in which conditions of temperature and humidity are carefully controlled.

The carpet is big, 34ft 3in long and 7ft 7in wide, and is covered in ornate decoration. It is a knotted carpet based on warp and weft of silk with wool knotting. Altogether ten different natural dyes have been used and there are 5,300 knots to a 10cm square. Making it must have been an immense task, involving it has been estimated as many as ten weavers, working over a number of years. The 'slave of the portal' was not literally a slave, but an expert who served the court and supervised the whole process. The central feature represents the dome of the mosque, with lanterns hanging from it. They are not the same size, and this could well be a deliberate imperfection. Carpet makers in Muslim countries still include deliberate 'mistakes' as an act of piety, since only Allah can produce perfection. This is as much a work of art as a mere floor covering.

It is not surprising that when Europeans saw such carpets, they wanted them to enrich their own grand houses and palaces. Turkey developed a successful export trade and Cardinal Wolsey made a present of over 200 carpets, nearly all from Turkey, to Henry VIII in the 1520s. As there were several portraits of the portly king standing on carpets, they created a demand for carpets for the wealthy and by the reign of Elizabeth I, carpets were being made in England. They were not necessarily, however, seen as floor coverings, no doubt because they were simply too expensive to stamp on, but were either hung up on walls for decoration or used as table covers. A painting of the peace negotiations between England and Spain held at Somerset House in 1604 shows the delegates ranged either side of a long table covered in an ornate carpet.

Carpet manufacture in Europe began in the late sixteenth century. The Aubusson factory started work in 1580 and was soon followed in c.1600 by a works established at Palais Royal, Paris by Pierre Dupont. The factory later moved to a former soap factory, hence the name Savonnerie from '*savon*' the French for soap. In 1627, the works were given a monopoly for making royal carpets by Louis XIII. The company trained staff through a rigorous apprenticeship scheme. Sixty orphans would be taken in and taught not only carpet making, but also design, and their artwork was assessed each month by a Member of the Académie. The carpets were noted for their exquisite workmanship and were made exclusively for the royal family, who occasionally passed them on as valuable diplomatic gifts. When Louis XIV came to the throne he initiated a programme of persecution of Protestants, known as Huguenots. Many fled to England, including workers from Savonnerie, who, not surprisingly, were warmly welcomed at Wilton, where carpet making had begun in 1655. Production continued to use the traditional techniques until late in the eighteenth century, when a new type of woven carpet was introduced, based on a technology first developed in Brussels.

Machine made carpets were introduced into Kidderminster in 1735. They were based on a draw loom, a device normally associated with silk manufacture, in which the warp threads were manipulated in the correct order by the draw boy to create ornate patterns. The weaving was complex, involving at least two worsted warp and two or more woollen weft. The weft threads were held in different shuttles and passed through the warp when needed to create the pattern. These were known as two-ply or double-cloth carpets and carried the same design on the front as they did on the back. They were not pile carpets as the knotted carpets being made at the time in Wilton and Axminster were, but they were cheaper. Later, this double-cloth carpet was improved on by the development of a triple-cloth in Kilmarnock in 1824. The carpets with intricate patterns were known as Brussels.

The Kidderminster carpets were made in factories, but with an arrangement that was unique. The tall draw looms were too big to fit into houses in the town, but the work was still done by self-employed handloom weavers. They had keys to the factory and could choose their own times to work. There was a long tradition of honouring 'Saint Monday' and taking the day off, making up the time later in the week by working longer hours. They were not paid wages but by the length of carpet completed. As in the silk industry, the weavers had to take on draw boys to manipulate the warp – though, in spite of the name, girls were also employed. Boys would have a two-year apprenticeship, after which they might become weavers. This was not an option for the girls, who when they finished working on the loom were given less skilled and lower paid jobs, such as bobbin winding. The workers often worked long hours – one weaver responding to a Commission's enquiries recalled some shifts of men working from 3am to 10pm. A regular feature was the back-to-back twenty-four hour shifts for two weavers, each working twelve hours.

In 1828, the factory owners cut the payment for weaving one yard of Brussels from 1s to 10d, at a time when 8 yards a day was considered an average output. In March, the weavers went on strike, and as often happened at this period, produced a rash of broadsheet ballads arguing the weavers' case. They were supported by the Rev. Humphrey Price, vicar of a parish near Lichfield, but who had been born in Kidderminster. He wrote a number of poems, painting a vivid picture of misery, with verses such as this:

Hush thee my babe! Thou wilt not see
Thy mother sick in misery;
Thy father too – all gone his bloom
And his heart's blood upon the loom.

As well as writing about the misery of the weavers, he also lambasted the wealth of the owners. This resulted is his being put on trial for criminal libel and receiving a one year jail sentence. It did not stop him from continuing to support radical causes and he was an enthusiastic supporter of parliamentary reform and the Chartist movement. The strike itself went on until August when, with funds exhausted, the weavers capitulated. The pay did go down to 10d and they were forced into the detested twelve backed by twelve hour working pattern.

Carpet making began in America in 1791, when William Sprague opened a works in Philadelphia, followed by other mills in New England. Carpet manufacture was about to be revolutionised, but not by someone working inside the

Manufacturing tufted carpets in Donegal c.1900.

industry. Erastus Bigelow was born in Massachusetts in 1814, the son of a cotton weaver who had hoped the boy would become a doctor. It turned out the money was not available for him to study medicine, but it was not a disaster, for he turned out to have an amazingly inventive mind. When he was just fourteen, he invented a machine for making piping cord, for which he was paid $100. More inventions followed and he also found time to write a manual on a system of shorthand. Then, in 1839 he invented a power loom for weaving double-cloth carpets. His first version produced up to 12 yards a day, but he made improvements and he was eventually able to produce 25 yards daily. His next improvement of 1849 was to produce a version with an added Jacquard attachment, to produce highly decorative Brussels carpets, the first of which were manufactured by the Clinton company of Massachusetts. The new loom was shown at a London exhibition in 1850. The Jacquard had already been in use in Kidderminster, but only for handlooms and now power loom jacquards came into use in Britain as well as in America.

There were many more improvements in carpet weaving in the nineteenth century, but the elaborate Brussels carpet had its limitations, being limited to six colours and the dyed worsted pile was very expensive. In 1832, Richard Whytock of Edinburgh invented a drum printing process, which he later improved on. The pile warp threads were wrapped round a printing drum and in its final form, the colours printed on the treads by means of a dye trolley running on rails under the drum. The tinted warp carpet had its pattern on the surface provided by the warp. The chenille carpet, invented by James Templeton and W. Quigley from Glasgow, was developed for a technique they had devised for weaving Paisley shawls. When the severed ends of the woollen weft were cut, they looked a bit like furry caterpillars – *chenilles* in French. James Templeton & Son was established as a carpet making company at Bridgeton on the east side of Glasgow. They specialised in pictorial carpets of great complexity, one of which, showing the twelve apostles, was exhibited in Paris in 1867. In 1889, a new factory was built on Glasgow Green, which is probably the most ornate factory in the whole of the British Isles. This was an important site, near the city centre, and several designs were rejected so the company turned to a leading Glasgow architect, William Leiper, already well known for several imposing Presbyterian churches in the fashionable Gothic style. His design was modelled on the Doge's Palace in Venice and is a riot of red and white brickwork set in diaper patterns and marble columns. The early history of the building was marked by two disasters. In 1899, during the construction of an extension next to a low level weaving shed, a high wind set a wall crashing down through the roof of the shed, where young women were at work and twenty-nine were killed. A year later, fire broke out, trapping and killing many more workers. Carpet making stopped in 1984 and the building is now a business centre.

By the end of the nineteenth century, carpet making had reduced the price to the point where they were no longer affordable only by the very rich. And thanks to changes in technology, richly patterned carpets were available to suit Victorian taste. At the end of a century, developments in rural America would eventually transform the carpet industry.

Catherine Evans was born to a farming family in Georgia, USA near the town of Dalton in 1880. As one of seven children, she was expected to help out on the farm and left school after just five years education. She later wrote, 'When I was a girl I wished that I had been a boy. Because a boy could find work to make money, and there was nothing a girl could do to earn money.' It turned out very differently. When she was twelve years old, she visited a cousin and saw a family heirloom, a white candlewick bedspread, in which there was a raised tufted pattern overlaying the basic material. She was so impressed that she taught herself the technique, which basically involved sewing dense threads into a material, so that loops emerged on one side that could then be cut. It is a very old technique but by then had largely been ignored. Neighbours admired her first effort and persuaded her to make bedspreads for them. They became so popular that she had to train up other local girls to help meet the demand. In 1917, she and her brother set up the Evand Manufacturing Company in Dalton, still employing girls working in their own homes. Their first big order in 1918 was for twenty-four bedspreads for a large department store in Atlanta. They added items such as tufted rugs to their bedspread business.

Other manufacturers soon sprang up in Dalton, all helped on their way with advice and details of patterns by Catherine. In the 1930s the first tufting machine was introduced, based on the Singer sewing machine, but with twelve needles in a row for tufting. Later this was improved on and machines were able to turn out bedspreads 56 inches wide. By the 1950s, the manufacture of tufted materials had included carpets, but still this was only ten per cent of the whole carpet production in America. It was, however, to grow rapidly in importance and tufting machines were also introduced into Europe. Hand tufted carpets had been made there for centuries, but the tufting machines brought huge changes. The introduction also coincided with the introduction of synthetic fibres, such as nylon. The combination of tufting machines and the new fabrics caused a catastrophic drop in demand for wool carpets. Dalton, where the young girl first decided to try and make a beautiful bedspread, is now known as 'The Carpet Capital of the World'. The town is responsible for around ninety per cent of the carpets sold in America. In Britain, tufted carpets also dominate the market: recent figures show an annual sale value of almost £700 million a year. A popular version of carpet available today is 80 per cent wool and 20 per cent nylon or similar synthetic.

Chapter Twelve

Tapestry

Tapestry is essentially a woven fabric in which the weft alone shows on the surface, generally showing a picture and often used as a wall hanging. Examples have been found in the tomb of Tutankhamun and examples can be seen from as far away as China and from pre-conquest Peru. The definition, however, excludes the 'tapestry' that is best known in Britain. The famous Bayeux tapestry showing the Norman invasion of 1066 is embroidered, not woven. Wall hangings, often with complex patterns, go back to ancient times. Some of the finest of these tapestries come from the Byzantine Empire and there is a particularly fine example now preserved in the Dumbarton Oaks Collection in Washington DC. The Hestia tapestry was woven in the sixth century and is made entirely of wool and shows the goddess of the hearth, Hestia, with two attendants and accompanying putti. It is comparatively small, just 114 by 136cm, compared with the later medieval tapestries, but the later versions were never just decorative items: they had a practical use as well.

The castles and grand houses of the princes and nobles scattered throughout Europe look romantic and grand, but with stone walls and only open fires for heat, they must have been depressingly cold in winter. Hanging material on the walls would act as insulation and if you are going to hang stuff up and you are rich, there is no reason why that hanging should not also be highly decorative. It not only looked good to the residents but would impress other visiting nobility if their hangings weren't quite as grand as yours. Kings and princes often had more than one royal residence, and their tapestries could be rolled up and taken with them on their travels in bags specially made for the job. Henry VIII was an enthusiastic commissioner of tapestries and ten of them were valued at his death at £5,000, which would be about half a million today – the richer you were, the richer your tapestry. It was not just individuals who commissioned work. Tapestries could also be used to express civic pride. The burghers of Tallinn, the current capital of Estonia, wanted a set of tapestries to show their importance. They were to be hung in the town hall, completed in 1404 and the oldest surviving town hall in Europe. Most had biblical themes, such as The Judgement of Solomon.

Manufacturing tapestries was to become a big and lucrative business. France and Flanders became important centres. The city of Arras in northern France had been at the heart of the wool trade since the eleventh century and by the fourteenth century had become such a prolific producer of tapestries that the name became synonymous with wall hangings. Its most famous literary reference comes in Hamlet, when the unfortunate Polonius hides behind the arras, only to be stabbed to death by Hamlet, who thinks he is killing Claudius. In France, Jean-Baptiste Colbert began organising the many ateliers spread around Paris, bringing all the weavers into one great complex of workshops, in the city bedside the River Bièvre, a tributary of the Seine. Its patron was Louis XIV, who commissioned many pieces, often glorifying his own reign – the 'Sun King' was never noted for his modesty. The complex was to become famous as the Gobelins factory. It is one of the best known of all the French manufacturers, but it is by no means unique. By the middle of the fifteenth century, it has been estimated there have been as many as 15,000 weavers working on tapestries in the Loire valley alone.

Visitors to the Gobelins factory c.1660 in an etching by Sebastian Leclerc.

The actual process of creating a tapestry begins with the design produced by an artist. This was usually in the form of a painting, known as a cartoon, from the Italian *cartone* or 'large paper' as the cartoons were the same size as the tapestries to be copied from them. Quite how the name came to be used for comic drawings and then animated films seems to be something of a mystery, for there was very little humour involved in most tapestries. In many cases, the design would have been the work of an artist employed by the manufacturer, but for the most expensive works, internationally famous artists could be employed. In 1515, Pope Leo X commissioned Raphael to produce a set of cartoons for ten tapestries depicting the lives of the saints Peter and Paul that were to hang in the Sistine Chapel in Rome, to complement the famous painted ceiling. Of the ten cartoons, seven survive and each is over three metres high, depicting lifesize figures. They are on display in the Victoria and Albert Museum in London.

In the seventeenth century, the centre for tapestry moved to what was then the Netherlands, with Brussels at the heart of it. Archduke Albert was now the most important patron, who commissioned cartoons from the leading artists of the day, notably Peter Paul Rubens. Unlike earlier artists, Rubens usually presented his cartoons not as works on paper, but as oil paintings on board. The style was baroque, full of colourful, dynamic imagery. In Britain, James I established the country's first tapestry works at Mortlake on the Thames in 1619. Instead of employing artists, most of the works were copies of old masters. His son Charles even bought seven of the Raphael cartoons – which is how they came to end up in the Victoria and Albert.

By the eighteenth century, tastes had changed again. The new fashion was known as Rococo and was even more elaborate than Baroque. The master of the genre was the French painter Francois Boucher. He was famous for voluptuous nudes and cavorting nymphs in romanticised pastoral scenery. He also painted some remarkably erotic works, quite unlike anything else being produced at the time. He was a favourite of the French court and many of his works were commissioned by the King's notorious mistress Madame Pompadour. Everything in his works was romanticised, full of milkmaids who would have been puzzled what to do if faced with a cow and shepherds who had never tended sheep. He worked as a cartoonist first at Beauvais and from 1755 at Gobelins. The cartoons are like his other paintings, exquisitely executed but hopelessly idealised. As the famous encyclopaedist Diderot wrote, 'That man can do anything – except tell the truth.' When you have cartoons produced by some of the greatest artists of the day, then turning those into tapestries is going to make huge demands on the weavers charged with the task.

Two basic types of loom were used, but in both cases, the weaver had to work from the back of the warp, using a variety of coloured threads, each covering only a part of the surface, not continuously, reaching right across the full width of the warp as in cloth weaving. In the cheaper versions, linen might be used for the warp, but the grander tapestries all used wool. The weft would also be wool but could also include silk and precious metal, such as gold thread. The Raphael tapestries used the latter, and when Rome was sacked in 1527, some of them were apparently burned, reputedly by the troops of Charles V, simply to recover the metal. This was not quite the catastrophe that would have been the case if they had been burning a set of Raphael paintings, since, as long as the cartoons existed, the tapestries could be remade.

When weaving with the upright loom, the warp threads would be suspended vertically. Because the weaver worked from what would become the back side of the finished work, a mirror had to be placed to show the front so that he could keep a check that he was accurately reproducing the cartoon. He – and tapestry weavers were always men in the early years – would need to be constantly checking the huge cartoon, to know what colour of thread and what length had to be added next to develop the overall picture. With the largest cartoons, they would often be cut into strips, and when working on the horizontal loom these would be placed below the warp, and could be seen through the threads by the weavers. This technique was used for the Raphael tapestries. Because only comparatively short threads were used, it was possible for several weavers to work at the same time on the larger pieces. This was just as well, as for the most complex patterns, a weaver could take a month to finish just one square metre. Each of the Raphael tapestries for example, at roughly 15 square metres, represents over a year's work.

Tapestry weaving at the Gobelins factory near Paris.

Among the earlier manufacturers to set up in business in Britain was the famous Gobelins Company, who opened a factory in Fulham High Road, London in the early years of the eighteenth century. The factory was taken over by Piere Parisot in 1753. He was a most unlikely entrepreneur, with a colourful career. He was ordained as a Capuchin monk in France and was sent off to India to a mission at Pondicherry. There he got into a serious dispute with the Jesuits over ritual and returned to France, where he put forward his own views rather too forcibly and greatly offended the Jesuits with his criticism. He would have hoped for support from his own order, but the Capuchins also denounced him, and he was forced to leave the country and settle in England. It was there that he became involved in tapestry and carpet making at a works in Paddington under the name Abbe Platel, though quite what his qualifications for the job were is by no means clear. His move to Fulham was financed by the Duke of Cumberland, but it was not a great success, closing after just ten years.

Hand made tapestry manufacture was revived in Britain as part of the Arts and Crafts movement led by William Morris, a deliberate rejection of machine-made goods and a return to what was seen as the purest form of design, the Gothic of the Middle Ages. Morris himself set up a small vertical tapestry loom in his bedroom in 1879 and completed his first tapestry there. In 1881, his company moved to Merton Abbey in South London, where they began commercially manufacturing tapestries. One of the leading artists employed was Edward Burne-Jones, a member of the Pre-Raphaelite Brotherhood, a group who, as its name suggests, looked back to the Middle Ages for inspiration. The business was a success, but paradoxically, the new tapestries were seldom bought by aristocrats to decorate their ancient manors, but by industrialists for their new houses.

The Gothic revival was just as strong in Scotland as it was in England, and owners of Scottish castles and grand houses were avid buyers of ancient tapestries. There was, however, no tapestry woven in the country until the Marquess of Bute brought two weavers from the Morris works to Edinburgh in 1912 at what became the Dovecot Tapestry works. They were given the task of weaving a work called 'The Lord of the Hunt' – a suitably Scottish scene, showing the Laird himself on horseback, surrounded by kilted Scots all looking at a dead stag. It was to be installed in his Gothic-revival pile Mount Stuart. It was to be 33ft long and 13ft 6in high, and the two weavers had apprentices to help. But all work came to a stop at the outbreak of war in 1914 – a war from which the weavers tragically were never able to return. In the event, the tapestry was finally hung in place in 1924.

'The Lord of the Hunt' was large but is dwarfed by a work produced in the twentieth century. The old Coventry Cathedral was destroyed by bombing in the Second World War and was replaced by a new, modern building. A number of artists were involved in designing stained glass and sculptures for the building and it was decided to commission a tapestry. The task of designing it went to Graham Sutherland in 1952 and he spent years working on the cartoon. He was more fortunate than his predecessors in that he did not have to produce a full-sized painting. Once the design was accepted, it was enlarged photographically. The finished work was to be a massive 23m by 12m and it was decided at the time that it would not be possible to find anyone in Britain who could weave such a work as a single piece. The job went instead to the French firm of Pinlon Frères, based near the famous tapestry centre of Aubusson. The work was carried out on a 500-year-old low loom. The warp threads were unbleached cotton spaced at twelve per inch, and the weft was wool from Australia. Altogether, 900 different shades were used in the work that took two years for twelve weavers to complete. It was unveiled at Coventry in 1962.

That was not the end of the story, however, for the Dovecot Tapestry works continued in business. They had hoped to be commissioned to produce the Sutherland tapestry, but they eventually received an even grander project. This was for a tapestry based on a painting by R.B. Kitaj for the new British Library being built in London. It is 6.75 by 6.75m, required 113kg of wool and took the seven weavers employed in making it a total of 7,000 person hours – unlike earlier woven tapestries, this was not an all-male workforce. It was completed in 1997 and was, for a time, the largest single-piece tapestry in the world, but was overtaken in 2018 by the 289 square metre tapestry made to celebrate the centenary of Espinar in Peru using a mixture of alpaca and sheep wool. A specially large, 16m long loom was used, with fifteen artisans at work on it. The world of big, woollen tapestries that seemed once to have died away completely has enjoyed a spectacular revival.

Chapter Thirteen

The Clothing Industry

Until the nineteenth century, once cloth left the mills, it went out either to be made into garments by tailors and seamstresses, or, with the inferior quality materials, to be worked up by the poorer classes in their own homes. In America, a survey of 1811 found that two thirds of all clothes worn in the country were made at home. The American ready-made clothing industry had two main markets. Planters were encouraged to buy clothes for their slaves, put together by poorly paid seamstresses in the north. It is a measure of the low pay of these women that the clothes were considered better value bought this way than allowing the slaves time off from working in the fields to make them for themselves. These would have been almost entirely cotton garments. The other main market at the time was clothing for sailors, made in just one size, which the sailor was expected to adapt to fit his own body. The increase in output of ready-made clothing would have scarcely been possible had everything relied on sewing by hand, but the early years of the century had seen mechanisation finally reach the garment industry. The new developments would make it possible to meet a growing demand for men's woollen suits and coats for both men and women.

The first patented sewing machine was developed in 1830 by a French tailor Barthélemy Thionnier that produced a chain stitch, in which the thread is passed through the fabric, pulled back through to create a loop, through which the thread is then passed – producing the series of chain-like links that give the stitch its name. The machine used a double, continuous thread and a special type of needle with the eye near the point. It does not ever seem to have gone into regular use. The first really practical sewing machine was designed by Elias Howe who was born in 1819 and at the age of sixteen was apprenticed to a cotton mill in Lowell, Massachusetts. In 1837 he moved to nearby Cambridge, working first on carding machines and then in 1839 working with a maker of precision instruments, Ari Davis. It was during his time there that he began thinking about a sewing machine, but apparently at first was baffled as he was trying to use a conventional needle with the point at one end and the eye at the other. According to family tradition, the answer came to him in a dream. He had been captured by a savage tribe whose king demanded he produce a sewing machine in a certain time or be put to death. He failed and was being taken away for execution when he noticed the warriors had holes near the points of their spears. He had his answer. A slightly more plausible explanation is that he had heard of the Thionnier machine.

The needle may have been similar to that of the earlier model, but the rest of the machine was different. For a start it produced a lock stitch, in which two threads were interwoven. It used a grooved needle and a shuttle on the other side of the cloth to pass the second thread through the first. It was patented in 1846. The lock stitch was to become the basis for future sewing machines. The Howe machine, however, did suffer from one big disadvantage – it could only be used to sew in a straight line. This problem was solved by a Michigan cabinet maker, Allen B. Wilson with his 'four-motion feed' that he patented in 1854. This was a toothed device that moved horizontally and advanced the material being sewn after each stitch. The cloth could be moved in any direction, which made it possible to create a curved seam. He had earlier patented another device with a rotary hook and bobbin that provided a circular movement to create the stitch, instead of the backward and forwards motion of the Howe machine.

This was the basis for the industrial sewing machine, that was later improved by Max Gritzner in Germany.

If there is one name, more than any other associated with the sewing machine, it is that of Singer.. To say that Isaac Singer had a colourful life would be a huge understatement. He was born in Pittstown, New York in 1811 and at the age of twelve he ran away from home to join a travelling theatre company. Later he left to work as a joiner and lathe operator. It was during this period that he patented a rock drill in 1839, a design that he sold to the Illinois and Michigan Canal Company for $2,000. With the money he went back to the world of theatre, changing his name to Merritt and forming the Merrit Players, leaving his wife to tour with his mistress who appeared as 'Mrs. Merritt'. The company kept going for five years, after which he turned back to invention. His new venture was for a wood block cutting machine, which turned out to not be a success. He was, however, working in a shop owned by Orson Phelps, who was selling and repairing sewing machines. These were made by Lerow and Blodgett, who had patented what they called a 'rotary sewing machine' that was operated by a hand crank. Phelps told Singer that it was a difficult machine to work with and Singer began to think of ways of improving it. His machine had a straight needle moving vertically and was operated by a foot treadle instead of the hand wheel. In many ways it was closer to the Howe model than to the Lerow and Blodgett, and Singer was obliged to pay part of his profits as a royalty to Howe for his patent.

The Singer machine was ideal for use in homes and when I.M. Singer & Co. went into production in 1856, they sold some 2,500 machines. This number had grown to 13,000 by 1860. It was a huge success and Singer began expanding to create a truly international business. By the time of his death he had made a fortune, leaving a legacy of $13 million to be divided between the twenty-six children that he acknowledged, born

The Singer sewing machine patent model of 1851.

to his first and second wives and more than one mistress. The company continued expanding internationally after his death and an immense new factory was opened on Clydebank near Glasgow. It was organised on a mass production basis and by 1911 was employing 12,000 workers, of whom 3,000 were women. The company was strongly anti-union and imposed harsh conditions on the workforce. In March of that year, the management cut the number of women working in the cabinet polishing department from fifteen to twelve, increasing their work load but with no extra pay. They stopped work and within days 10,000 Singer workers were on strike in support of their claim. Eventually the strike was settled by a ballot, but one in which the voters names and addresses were on the voting papers and the company made it quite plain that they would not take a very kind view of anyone voting to stay out. In spite of the implied threat, over 4,000 voted to stay out, but the majority, who had long since run out of funds, voted to return. The strike leaders lost their jobs and there was widespread victimisation of those who had supported strike action. It paved the way for the area becoming known as 'Red Clyde' in later years. Singer has continued to produce sewing machines from factories around the world and became the leading manufacturers of machines for home use. It was, however, to be the rotary machines of Wilson and Gritzner that were to prove the greatest importance in the clothing industry and attract the attention of the woollen cloth industry.

The availability of efficient sewing machines gave rise to a new, thriving industry in ready-made clothing. Other inventions of the nineteenth century helped to improve the efficiency of the process. In 1859, the band saw used for cutting very thin slices of timber for veneers was adapted by converting the saw blade to a knife. This was then used to cut multiple layers of cloth. In 1888 Jacob Bloch developed the first electrically powered cutting machine that used a circular knife. In the same year he designed another electric cutter, this time with a straight blade that moved up and down. Economy was improved in 1897 when James Marsden developed his lay-marking process. Traditionally the lines to be cut by tailors were marked on the cloth in chalk. Templates for the different parts of the garment were made using light card, in which holes were punched to give the outline of the pattern. These were laid out to make the maximum use of the material. When that was done, chalk dust was sprinkled over the cards, passing through the perforations to leave the chalk marks on the material. By the 1950s, photographic methods were used to analyse the best use of material, a job that today would be computerised.

Major changes in the American industry really got under way with the outbreak of the Civil War which created a demand for huge quantities of woollen uniforms. The Union conscripts were all measured and had uniforms made to fit. The information gained from these measurements enabled clothing to be produced in a range of standard sizes. Over the years, more surveys produced more statistics. During the First World War, the American army took measurements from 1,000 recruits to help make appropriate uniforms, which improved the accuracy of the information available, but the Civil War records were sufficient to start the process and encourage the development of the industry.

In Britain, the first big emporium selling ready-made clothing was opened by Elias Moses and his son in the 1840s in Aldgate, London. By the 1850s other large stores had opened, all employing out workers to produce their stock. It has been estimated that by the 1850s the main stores between them were employing over 3,000 in sweat shops in the East End of London. As in New York, the vast majority of these low-paid workers were Jewish.

One manufacturer, who was to become a major player, was Hepworth's, and they travelled in the opposite direction – moving from manufacturer to store owner. Joseph Hepworth was born in 1834 at Lindley, near Huddersfield, where his father worked as a cloth dresser. Like most children at that time, he left school at an early age to join his father at the mill. He married in 1855, still a mill worker and in the 1860s, was living with his mother-in-law. The family connection proved useful, as with his brother-in-law, James Rhodes, he was able to start a business in Leeds making 'juvenile clothing'. Rhodes soon retired, and Joseph's son Norris joined the firm. By 1871, this was quite a small concern, with just twenty-three employees, but was growing and by 1890 they had both a factory and a large number of outworkers, with a total workforce of around three hundred. It was Norris who made the fundamental change. He realised that they could make more money if, instead of selling their clothes to a shop keeper, they opened their own shops and decided that to make a real impact they needed to do so in several big towns at once. By 1891 they had eighty-one shops all round the country and a new factory in Leeds. They dominated the ready-made market until the early twentieth century when a rival appeared.

The next story starts in 1900, when fifteen-year-old Moshe Osinsky left Russia to escape the pogroms that were terrorising the Jewish population. He was an entrepreneur from a young age, and in 1903, while still just 18 years old, he borrowed £100 from a relative and set up in business selling ready-made clothing. He married in 1909 and by the outbreak of the First World War he had expanded his business in both making and selling men's clothing, with works in Leeds and 14 shops. The shops, however, were not called Osinsky's. By now he had acquired an English name – he was Montague Burton. In the war years he was kept busy making uniforms. Over the next few years, the business continued to grow, helped by a successful advertising campaign – he became famous as providing the 'Five guinea suit for 55 shillings' (£5 5s suit for £2 15s). In 1921 he opened a new factory in Leeds, built in the fashionable Art Deco style that was soon employing 10,000 workers and turning out an astonishing 30,000 suits a week. It was the biggest clothes factory in the world at that time. Unlike the unhappy workers in the sweatshops, the Burton workers enjoyed a remarkably good working environment. The staff canteen seated 8,000 workers. Burton provided a full free medical service for the staff, including dentistry and podiatry. His Christmas parties for the staff were famous; there was a present for every child of every employee.

The idea of setting up clothing factories near to woollen mills was not limited to West Yorkshire. The same thing happened in Gloucestershire and Stroud which stands at the heart of five valleys, each supporting a string of mills was the obvious site. Holloways had two factories, one of which, in Brick Row, was devoted to making suits from local cloth – the other was known locally as 'the shirt factory'. It was established in 1849 by two brothers, George and Henry Holloway, and

The machinists' room at the C.W.S. clothing factory at Batley.

was to become the biggest employer in the town, at its height providing work for 1,000 people. Originally steam power was used to work the sewing machines, but this was later replaced by Singer machines, each fitted with its own electric motor. By the time of its closure in 1975, there were just some eighty workers there. A second works was built next to the railway station in 1898 but worked on a smaller scale. In 1902 it was taken over by Hill Paul, but like Holloways no longer works. The Holloways buildings have gone, but Hill Paul remains, converted into apartments, with the addition of an extra floor to provide two penthouse flats.

There is a personal note that ties me into this part of the story. Although there was expertise in cloth making in Stroud, there was no great tradition of clothing manufacture so, as other clothing companies did, Holloways brought in Jewish workers, mostly from London. They formed quite a large community, but the nearest synagogue was in Cheltenham. In 1879 a temporary synagogue was established on Slad Road, but when funds were available a permanent building

The former Hill Paul clothing factory at Stroud, now converted into apartments. The penthouse top is a later addition.

was completed in 1889. The timing was not good: the local cloth industry was in decline and the Jewish population was drifting away. By 1909, there were not enough left to keep the synagogue viable and the building was sold off and converted into two semi-detached three-storey houses. And one of those houses has been my home for nearly thirty years. It is rather appropriate that I have been writing this chapter, almost entirely concerned with the contribution made by the Jewish community to the clothing industry of Britain in a synagogue paid for by clothing workers.

Chapter Fourteen

Development and Decline

Changes in technology continued to affect the wool industry from the middle of the nineteenth century. Mule spinning remained normal in many factories, but the throstle was in need of adaptation to make it really efficient. The biggest problem was with the flyer, the part that spun round to twist the wool. It had to be removed in order to change the bobbins and then be replaced. The first solution was the ring frame, developed in America in the late 1820s to early '30s. Yarn from the rollers passes through a guide ring. It is then attached to a wire ring, the traveller, that fits round the ring that gives the machine its name. The ring fits over the spindle holding the bobbin. As the ring rotates it takes the traveller with it and twists the wool. The spun yarn is wound onto the bobbin and the ring itself moves up and down to ensure the yarn is applied uniformly. It was to find a limited use in the woollen industry. At much the same time, Charles Danforth developed another way of avoiding the flyer problem that he patented in America in 1828. In this version, a rotating cap was placed around the spindle carrying the bobbin and the yarn passed under the cap before being wound on. By the 1850s, the cap spinning frame had been widely adopted for worsted spinning.

There were major changes, too, in the preparatory stages, especially with combing, where a number of different machines were developed. The Noble-Donisthorpe circular comb of the 1850s came into general use in America and in Yorkshire. The Holden-Lister square comb worked much more like the hand comb, with three separate sets of combs, and came into regular use in the French worsted industry, but

Ring frame spinning machinery at the Museum of Science and Industry in Manchester.

its use in Britain was mainly confined for use with the finest merino wool.

In the twentieth century a wholly new type of spinning machine was developed, known as open end. It came into operation in the 1960s, though a similar system had been patented as early as 1937 in Denmark. The fibres are fed to an opening device and are carried along on an air stream into a cup-shaped rotor that could be revolving at speeds up to 60,000 revolutions a minute. The fibres collect in grooves on the inside of the cup, gradually being built up and when they are peeled off, the rotor provides the twist. The period also saw the development of a variety of shuttleless looms. The Sulzer Organization of Switzerland began the commercial development of one type which used a small projectile that grasped thread from a pack at the side of the loom and shot across the loom to the opposite side, where the yarn is clamped and the end cut. An alternative version is the rapier version, in which the two rapiers move simultaneously from each side to meet in the centre, when the one carrying the thread transfers it to the other. In the most recent versions, the mechanical element has disappeared altogether, and the weft is carried across on an air jet. The great advantage of these systems is not just in increased speed of operation, but that it is continuous. There is no need to stop to remove a shuttle to insert more thread.

It was not only machinery that changed over the years. The manufacture of chemical dyes has a curious history. Manufacturers would have liked to have alternatives to the often soft colours produced from natural materials, but had no idea how to make them. This is because the organic molecules that are produced in these dyes are very complex: a non-organic molecule, like the inorganic common salt we use in cooking has only two atoms per molecule, but the organic sugar we also use has 45 atoms per molecule. The story begins with August Wilhelm von Hofmann, who, although born in Germany, became head of the newly formed Royal College of Chemistry in London in 1845. He took the complex coal tar and began using distillation techniques to produce a variety of different organic compounds, one of which was benzene, which, when mixed with nitric acid, produced aniline, a name that comes from the Portuguese word *'anil'* that in English is indigo – which is, of course, a well-known dye. But the chemists were looking for quite different applications. They were quite specifically looking for ways to manufacture valuable drugs. One compound they produced was allyl-toluidine that had a structure similar to quinine, then used to treat malaria. One of Hofman's assistants, William Perkin, tried treating allyl-toluidine with potassium dichromate and sulphuric acid in order to add an extra oxygen atom to create something closer to quinine. All he got was a sludgy mess, so he tried again, this time with aniline and again he got a black sludge. He tried boiling it with water and this time he got a pleasant, purplish liquid that formed into crystals. He thought it looked very attractive and decided to try to use it to dye a piece of silk. The cloth retained the colour and didn't fade. He sent off a sample to a firm of dyers in Perth and received an enthusiastic response: 'This colour is one that has been wanted in all classes of goods.' Perkins was encouraged, and with financial help from his father set up a dye works near Harrow in 1857. It was first known, prosaically as 'aniline purple' but when the colour became popular in France, it was renamed mauve. When Queen Victoria attended the Great Exhibition at the Crystal Palace in a mauve silk dress, the colour became instantly fashionable. It was the first of the aniline dyes and gave birth to a whole new industry making a wide range of artificial dyes.

Although many new technologies were being developed, that does not mean that they were adopted throughout the industry. In Britain, in particular, many mills still relied on older machinery, largely because they had considerable market protection through the extended Empire. New competitors were, however, starting to appear. China opened its first woollen mill in the 1870s during the Qing dynasty, using material from local sheep. The wool itself was quite coarse, but as most of the manufacturing was for military uniforms, this was not a major problem. In 1894, a Chinese-Australian merchant Quong Tart visited China to try to persuade them to buy the superior quality merino wool from Australia. He did not have a lot of success. However, the end of the Qing dynasty and the growth of the Chinese Nationalist Party in the 1930s brought about many changes. There was a campaign encouraging women to knit, arguing that it was their patriotic duty and would help in the modernisation of China. Shanghai became an important centre and gradually the trade that Quong Tart had hoped to develop between Australia and China became increasingly important. Australia encouraged investment in the Chinese industry, and it began to grow rapidly through the 1930s. A survey of Chinse mills in 1933 recorded 7,600 spindles: by 1937 that had grown to 42,352 spindles. Initially, China had imported all its machinery, mainly from European manufacturers, but with a rapidly developing iron and steel industry they were soon able to manufacture everything for themselves. Today, China has its own sheep farms but still imports huge quantities of wool from Australia and is now the biggest manufacturer of wool yarn in the world, most of it going to the domestic market, but also having sufficient capacity to create a healthy export trade.

The development of artificial fibres has a long and complex history. It began with the idea of making artificial silk, and one scientist, a Swiss chemist called George Audumans, reasoned that if the silk worm could make the real thing from mulberry leaves, it should be possible to use scientific methods to get the same result. He tried treating the bark and succeeded in producing fibres, but the process was so complex that it turned out to be more efficient to let the silk worm do its thing after all. The next logical step was to discover what chemical was involved and, as it seemed unlikely that the mulberry was fundamentally different from other plants, it would be common to many. Eventually, it was discovered that they key chemical was cellulose, which consisted of long chains of glucose molecules. Various scientists began experimenting with cellulose and the big breakthrough came when a manufacturer of billiard balls offered a $10,000 award for anyone who could make artificial ivory. John Wesley Hyatt decided to take up the challenge and began working with cellulose nitrate. When he treated it with a mixture of camphor and ethanol. he produced a flexible substance that he called celluloid. It was not suitable for billiard balls, but it found a market in making cuffs that could be worn by clerks and could be wiped clean when they got stained with ink. It was the first successful plastic.

Nitrocellulose proved useful in producing a variety of other materials, and one of those who began working on it was the extravagantly named Louis-Marie Hilaire Bernigaut de Grange, Comte de Chardonnet, who had worked with Pasteur. He became interested in silk and the possibility of making an artificial version. He succeeded thanks to an accident. Nitrocellulose had been used to create gun cotton and when that was dissolved in a mixture of ether and alcohol it produced a transparent material when dried called collodion that was used to cover photographic plates. Chardonnet was working with liquid collodion in his dark room, when he knocked the bottle over. When he tried to wipe up the mess, it formed long filaments. It was the breakthrough he had been looking for, and he developed a new material 'Chardonnay silk' that went into production in 1891. The name was a bit cumbersome, and someone suggested that because it shimmered in rays of light it could be called rayon – the name stuck. With this initial success, it was inevitable that others would start to work on producing a wider range of synthetic fibres.

Leading the search for new materials was the Du Pont Company. They set up research groups within the chemistry department in the 1920s, specifically to look for new polymers. Their most famous success was nylon, marketed in 1938, originally for toothbrush bristles, but was soon adapted to making stockings. The name was chosen with rayon in mind – the 'nyl' at the start were apparently chosen at random – it was not, as urban myth has it, a reference to New York and London. The outbreak of war brought a pause in this type of research, but the 1950s saw the emergence of new polymers such as acrylic and polyester. These were cheaper than the traditional natural fibres and soon became very popular for clothing.

Many factors combined to reduce the demand for woollen garments. Fashions had changed, with lighter materials being favoured in place of the heavier broadcloths. The blanket industry was badly hit by the change to duvets. The new fibres often replaced wool – or were mixed with it. In either case, the quantity needed was steadily coming down. In the carpet industry, tufting machines were first developed in the 1920s producing comparatively narrow material. Steady improvements made it possible to make carpets up to 5m wide, and artificial velour proved the ideal material for the machines. A modern machine would have as many as 2,500 needles and working together produce 120 million stitches an hour. There is still a demand for high quality woollen knotted carpets, but they have now become luxury items. One area where wool has thrived and demand grown throughout the twentieth century is for knitting wool for use at home – either with traditional needles or with knitting machines. But in the traditional woollen textile industries of countries such as Britain, the decline has been catastrophic. The effect of the decline in demand has had an even more dramatic effect on the primary producers in Britain. In 1955, sheep farmers were getting £14 per kilogram for their fleeces; by 2015, the price had plummeted to less than £1. Sheep farming is still a big industry – 45,000 farms, home to over 30 million sheep. Out of all these, only one farmer stocks merinos. The industry is almost entirely geared to meat production, not wool – the price paid scarcely covers the cost of shearing. But sheep have to be sheared, and Britain does produce around 70,000 tonnes of wool a year.

The decline in the industry was already severe by the early years of the twentieth century. In a debate in the House of Commons in 1930, it was reported that 476 woollen businesses had closed since 1918. The closures have not been uniform across Britain. The West of England cloth industry has all but disappeared, with the exception of the billiard cloth manufacturer, while in Wales the number of working mills has fallen from 250 in 1926 to just nine commercial mills today. Scotland has suffered similar declines. In the Border area, where the main industry developed, the emphasis has moved from cloth making to knitwear. Of twenty-seven working establishments, some of which are quite small, only five produce cloth, the rest are all knitting. There are surviving outliers, such as the cloth mill on Islay and the still thriving Harris Tweed industry. Yorkshire mills that once dominated

The end of an era: the chimney is all that remains of this mill in Keighley, demolished in 1984.

the world market have been hardest hit, simply because of their dominance, but there are signs of optimism here, with new investment. One example is Laxtons, a company founded by George Laxton in 1907, which was notable for innovation, in particular for producing a lightweight mohair. The business moved out of Britain but has since returned to Yorkshire in a brand new factory equipped with all the latest spinning machinery. One of their specialities is worsted yarn, using British wool. Their success is their ability to produce yarns specially designed to meet individual clients' requirements.

Is there a future for the woollen industry in the traditional areas where it developed? In recent years, there has been a movement away from an over-reliance on plastics and their effect on the environment. Natural materials are seen as far less harmful, but it seems unlikely that this will lead to a huge shift in manufacturing in places such as Britain when there has been such intensive development in other parts of the world. And the environmental argument has been something of a two-edged sword, some arguing that sheep farming is one of the villains in the battle against climate change. The history of wool is a long one and for a time was a vital element in Britain's prosperity. It will almost certainly never have the same central importance again, but sheep will still graze, yarn will be spun and knitted or woven to keep us clothed.

Gazetteer

Listed below are a number of sites including museums and working mills open to the public in Britain, with a selection of other sites in mainland Europe.

Bolton Museums: Bolton Steam Museum, Mornington Road, Bolton BL1 4EU. A former mill housing the extensive collection of mill engines of the Northern Mill Engine Society. *Nmes.org*. Hall i' th' Wood: the former home of Samuel Crompton, inventor of the spinning mule. *boltonlams.co.uk/hall-i-th-wood*.

Part of the Northern Mill Engine Society's collection of mill engines at their Bolton museum

Bradford Industrial Museum, Moorside Mills, Moorside Road, Eccleshall, Bradford BD2 3HP. Housed in a former worsted spinning mill, the museum has an imposing collection of textile machinery. *bradfordmuseums.org/bradford-industrial-museum.*

Carloway Mill, Carloway, Isle of Lewis. A working tweed mill and visitor centre. *thecarolowaymill.com*

Cold Harbour Mill, Uffculme, Cullompton, Devon EX15 3EE. A former woollen mill with both spinning and weaving and both water and steam power originally. Engines steamed on special days. *coldharbourmill.org.uk*

Colne Valley Museum, Cliffe Ash, Golcar, Huddersfield HD7 4PY. Traditional weavers' cottages with handloom. *colnevalleymuseum.org.*

Framework Knitters Museum, Chapel Street, Ruddington, Nottingham NG11 6HE. The museum demonstrates framework knitting in original workshops with workers' housing. *frameworkknittersmuseum.org*

Helmshore Textile Mills Museum, Holcombe Road, Helmshore, Rossendale BB4 4N8. Unusual in having both a fulling mill and a cotton mill on the same site – an excellent collection of historic machinery.*lancashire.gov.uk/leisure-and-culture/museums/helmshore-mills-textile-museum*

Knockando Woolmill, Abelour, Moray AB38 7RP. A working spinning and weaving mill. *kwc.co.uk*

Leeds Industrial Museum, Canal Road, Leeds LS12 2QF. The museum has an extensive collection, housed in the former Armley Mills, covering both the woollen and clothing industries. *museumsandgalleries.leeds.gov.uk/leeds-industrial-museum.*

Maison des Canuts, 10/12 rue d'Ivry 69004 Lyon, France. Although Lyon is famous for silk, the museum demonstrates every stage in the preparation and use of the Jacquard loom. *maisondescanuts.fr*

Manufacture des Gobelins, 47 Avenue de Gobelins, 75013 Paris. Guided tours of the famous tapestry manufacturer and exhibitions of tapestries. *visitparisregion.com/en/products/guided-tour-of-the-gobelins-manufactory*

Museo del Tessuto (Textile Museum) Via Puccetti 3- 59180, Prato, Italy. Housed in a former mill, the museum demonstrates every stage of textile production. *museodeltessuto.it*

Museum of Carpet, Stour Vale Mill, Green Street, Kidderminster DY10 1AZ. The museum is home to both machinery and a carpet design collection. *museumofcarpet.org.*

Nailsworth Mills: There are two sites, both operated by the Stroudwater Textile Trust. Dunkirk Mill, Stroud Road, Nailsworth Gl5 5HH demonstrates cloth finishing using machinery powered by a waterwheel. The Gig Mill, Old Bristol Road, Nailsworth GL6 0JB has hand- and power looms. *stroudwatertextiletrust.org.uk*

National Wool Museum, Dre-fach Felindre, Felindre, Llandysul, Carmarthenshire SA44 5UB. This is both a museum and a working woollen mill. *museum.wales/wool.*

Newtown Textile Museum, 5-7 Commercial Street, Newtown, Powys SY16 2BL A museum showing the working life of handloom weavers. *newtowntextilemuseum.co.uk*

Solva Woollen Mill, Middle Mill, Solva, Haverfordwest SA62 6XD. A working weaving mill. *solvawoollenmill.co.uk*

Texteil Museum, Goir Kestraat 96, 5046 GN, Tilberg, Netherlands. The museum contains both working machinery and displays of historical textiles. *texteilmuseum.nl*

Trefriw Woollen Mill, Main Road, Trefriw LL27 0NQ. A working mill with all processes from fleece to cloth – machinery using electrical power from the mill's own water turbine powered generator. *t-w-m.co.uk*

Acknowledgements

I would like to thank the following for providing illustrations for this book. Every effort has been made to contact copyright holders for works in copyright.

Central News Photo Service, p.10; Clem Rutter, 168; Clive Coote, 109; Dave Bevins, 124; De Facto' 164; Dosseman, 145; Hans Brisbane Dick Fund, 165; John Fielding, colour section p.1, top; Joseph Mischyshyn, 138; Kirklees Cultural Services, 132; Lawrence Pan, 138; Leeds City Museum, colour section p.2, bottom; Metropolitan Museum of Ary, New York, 161; Mick Orr, 98; Museum of English Rural Life, 24; Northen Mill Engine Society, 176; Rosser, 154; Royal Commission etc, 174; South Australia Archive, 15; Stroudwater Textile Trust, 84, 89, 111, 121; Sushma Shama, 31; Time Green, colour section p.5, top; Trinity Cambridge, 36; V & A49, colour section p.1, bottom; West Yorkshire, 103; William Lawrence, 151.

Select Bibliography

Aspen C. & Chapman, S.D., *James Hargreaves and the Spinning Jenny*, 1964

Benson, Anna & Warburton, Neil, *Looms and Weaving*, 1986

Blair, John & Ramsay, Nigel, *English Medieval Industries*, 1991

Blythell, Duncan, *The Handloom Weavers*, 1969

Burt, Steven & Grady, Kevin, *The Merchants' Golden Age, Leeds 1700-1790*, 1987

Butt, John, *The Industrial Archaeology of Scotland*, 1967

Campbell, Thomas P., *How Medieval and Renaissance Tapestries Were Made*, 2008

Cowgill, John, *An Historical Account of the Luddites*, 1862

Crump, N.B & Charbel, Gertrude, *History of the Huddersfield Woollen Industry*, 1935

Defoe, Daniel, *A Journey through the whole Island of Great Britain*, 1724-6

Dyer, John, *The Fleece*, 1757

English, W., *The Textile Industry*, 1969

Giles, Colum & Goodall, Ian H., *Yorkshire Textile Mills*, 1992

Harris, Jennifer (ed.) *5,000 Years of Textiles*, 1993

Hills, Richard L., *Power from Steam*, 1989

Horn, Pamela, *Labouring Life in the Victorian Countryside*, 1976

Leadbetter, Eliza, *Spinning and Spinning Wheels*, 1979

Mann, J, de L., *The Cloth Industry in the West of England*, 1971

Midgley, Thomas, *The Spinning Mule*, 1927

Origo, Iris, *The Merchant of Prato*, 1957

Palmer, Marilyn & Neaverson, Peter. *The Textile Industry of South-West England*, 2005

Rees, D. Morgan, *Industrial Archaeology of Wales*, 1975

Singer, Charles et al. (ed.) *A History of Technology* (7 volumes) 1954-78

Tann, Jennifer, *Wool and Water*, 2019

Ure, Andrew, *The Philosophy of Manufacture*, 1835

Index